The Unguidebook
Perth & Western Australia

A Picture Is Worth 1,000 Characters™

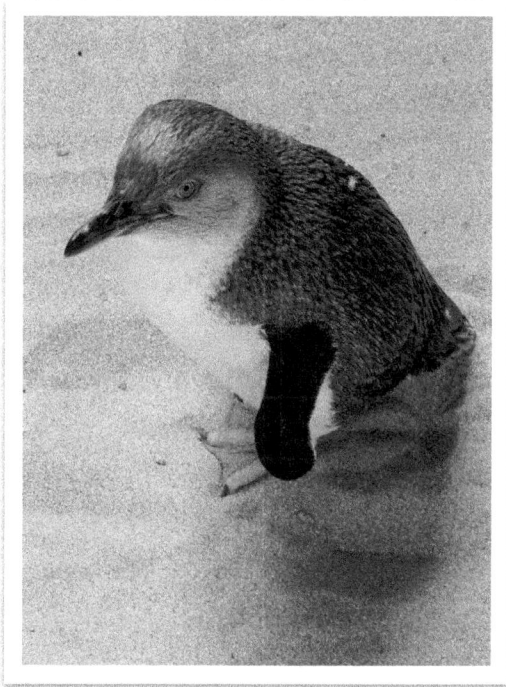

Cover photo of Natural Bridge in Kalbarri National Park.

Inside front photo of a fairy penguin at Penguin Island's Discovery Centre.

The Unguidebook™ Perth & Western Australia —
A Picture Is Worth 1,000 Characters™

© 2019 text and photographs by K. MacKenzie Freeman and Douglas J. Freeman

ISBN 9781674146201
Imaginexxus, Lake Oswego, OR 97035
www.imaginexxus.com

Created in the United States of America.

For Robyn and Jim,

*Libby and Oz may be worlds apart,
but nothing has kept us apart.
Thank you so much for sharing
your corner of the world with us.*

Travel around the world with our series:

The Unguidebook™ Hong Kong & Macau

The Unguidebook™ New Zealand's South Island

The Unguidebook™ Perth

The Unguidebook™ Perth & Western Australia

The Unguidebook™ Sydney

The Unguidebook™ Sydney & Melbourne

These books are available through these online sites: Amazon, Apple Books, Barnes & Noble and Imaginexxus.

Preface

Perth and the other towns in Western Australia are a *long* way from everything, and to some extent even each other.

One of the first things we discovered about this state was that the people who live here take full advantage of the gifts that nature has placed on their doorstep. This approach to life may be due to the region's remoteness or the Aussie spirit of living every day to its fullest or a combination of the two.

The sixth volume in our series, *The Unguidebook Perth & Western Australia,* will introduce you to these fun-loving people, the area's distinct scenery and many of its fascinating places. This book is similar to our others, in that it features original photographs and tales following our theme, *A Picture Is Worth 1,000 Characters.* These tales are exactly 1,000 characters long, down to the last period. Our goal is to help give you a sense of place rather than a checklist of what to see and do.

We gathered the material for this book while we were temporary residents in this incredible state. Though our living here for six weeks didn't make us experts on this region, we hope the insight we gained will help make your visit more enjoyable.

No matter if you spend six days or six weeks here, we think *The Unguidebook Perth & Western Australia* will help you understand why it's worth the trip to one of the most remote parts of the world.

Table of Contents

Perth

Fremantle

Just Outside of Town

Headed North

A Few Hours South

Authors' Note

It didn't take us long to learn that Aussies love to abbreviate all types of words. We were already familiar with *g'day* (good day) and *barbie* (barbeque), however we quickly discovered there are dozens of other abbreviated words that are a part of everyday Aussie speech. For example, people start their day with *brekkie* (breakfast) but at lunch might have a *bickie* (an English biscuit or an American cookie). We think Aussies don't abbreviate words out of laziness, but because they tend to be an easy-going, fun-loving lot and this attitude carries over into how they speak.

One of the most common abbreviations in this area is *WA* (the state of Western Australia). We try to avoid most abbreviations in our writing. However, we decided to occasionally employ this one because Aussies frequently use it and when we only have 1,000 characters for each story, every character matters. The use of this popular two-character abbreviation instead of the entire 17-character name allowed us to squeeze just a little bit more information into several stories. *Ta*! (Thank you!)

Perth

Walking in the Park

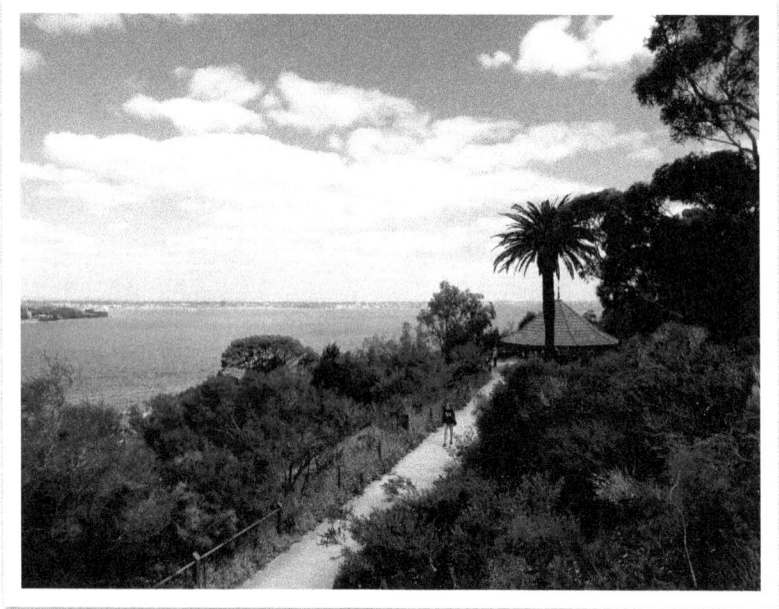

Regal Overlook

A unique way to get the lay of the land is to stroll through Kings Park. This urban sanctuary ranks as one of the world's largest and features drop-dead gorgeous views of the city.

It's home to 3,000 species of the state's flora and fauna, including a 750-year-old boab that was saved during a road construction project in the Kimberly. Because boabs are significant to the Aboriginal people, seeds from this particular tree were returned to their home and transplanted.

Throughout the park are various cultivated landscapes and walkways, but two-thirds of it is set aside for bushlands. These informal forests allow urban dwellers to escape into nature, just a few minutes' drive from downtown. And part of that drive involves passing through one of the country's living tributes to its war heroes. The avenues have been lined with eucalyptus trees, each dedicated to a serviceman who was killed or injured.

This place offers more than a respite. It also provides a primer to the spirit of this region.

Playground History Lesson

One of Western Australia's claims to fame is that Earth's oldest evidence of life has been found here in rocks and fossils that are nearly 3.5 billion years old. Larger life forms, like the phytosaur, date back to much more recent times such as the Triassic period, about 200 million years ago.

It's obvious from the phytosaur's armor-like skin, menacing eyes and overbite which no orthodontist could fix, that he's related to the modern-day crocodiles and alligators. Fortunately, there are no real phytosaurs alive today. And their cousin, the saltwater crocodile, can only be found in various rivers, estuaries and billabongs within the northwestern section of the state around Exmouth and Onslow.

This colossal phytosaur replica lies in wait near the May Drive Parkland's lake in Kings Park. Children adore the chance to clamber all over him and traipse along his rigid spine. Though he mainly serves as a play structure, he's also a reminder of this region's history and what remnants still exist.

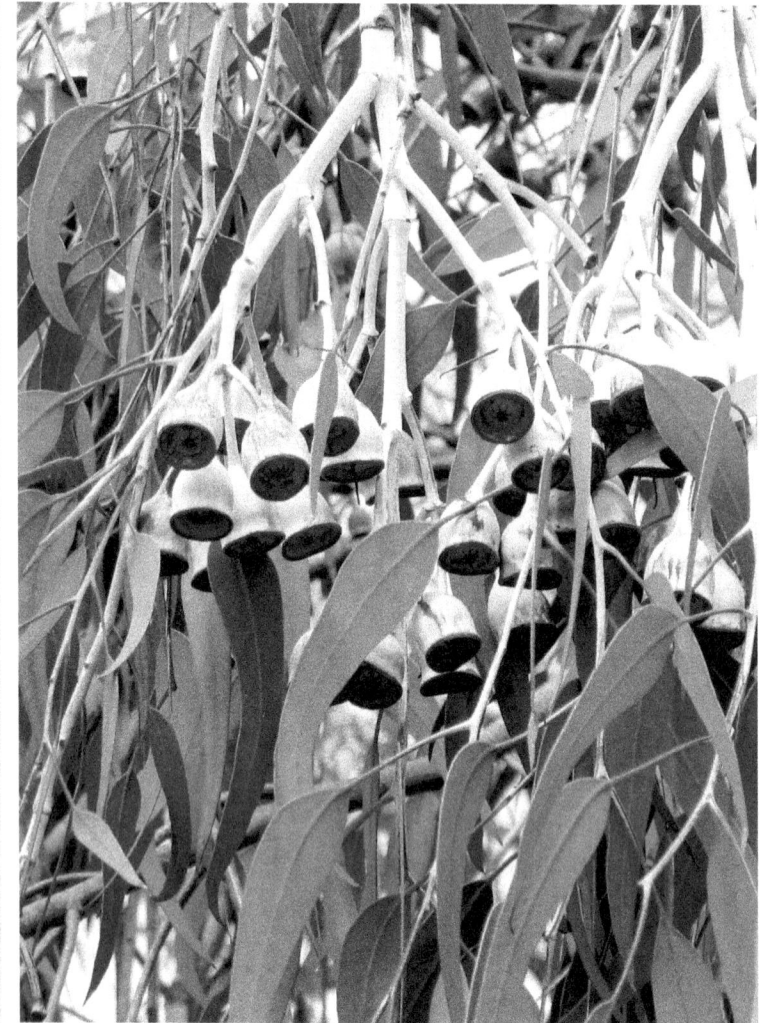

Decked out Gum Trees

Children tend to draw the world as they see it. And since the eucalyptus comprises three-fourths of Australia's native forest, chances are this type of tree would be featured prominently in most Aussie kids' artwork.

There are well over 700 species of eucalyptus, of which dozens are featured in Kings Park. Some are huge bushes. Others rank among the world's tallest trees. These myrtle family members have been a part of the Australian landscape since the Miocene epoch, 21 million years. And though the terrain has changed from prehistoric times, these trees are still found along much of the country's coastline and throughout Tasmania.

Almost all eucalyptus are evergreens and sport showy flowers that reminded us of designer drapery tassels suspended from woody pods. We noticed that this particular tree seemed to be decorated ahead of the holidays with its green leaves, red petioles and white bell-like ornaments. It could be the perfect subject for a drawing of a truly Aussie Christmas tree.

City Kangaroo Hop

A short walk from Perth's city center is Heirisson Island, a three million square foot cucumber-shaped refuge that sits smack in the middle of the Swan River. This was once a hunting ground for the Noongar people and is now home for a colony of western grey kangaroos.

We walked around the islet in hopes of spotting the marsupials. All of a sudden, two brown heads popped out of the waist-high grass. We instantly realized that their name was a misnomer because the color of their fur can vary and these two were unmistakably not grey.

This duo seemed indecisive as to what to do next. It was a warm afternoon and they were in absolutely no hurry to do much of anything. Eventually they hopped out into the open just a few feet away from us. Neither of them bounded like in the cartoons. Mosey would be a better way to describe how they moved. One wandered toward a tree to rest. The other was much more interested in lunch than us. Today's menu: a mixture of grasses with yellow blossoms on the side.

The Four-hour Day

The chance to see a koala is an amazing, but unfortunately rare opportunity. There are less than 100,000 living wild in the Australian bush and no more than a few hundred in zoos around the world.

To see a koala actually awake is an even more extraordinary experience. These cuddly looking marsupials sleep on average 20 hours a day. And the reason for their excess slumber is somewhat of a Catch-22. Their diet primarily consists of eucalyptus leaves which are high in toxins and fiber, but low in nutrition. Thus, they must consume vast quantities to attain enough fuel which requires an exorbitant amount of energy to digest. There's little time left in the day for anything other than chomping on leaves or snoozing.

We felt lucky to observe this doe and her seven or eight-month old joey at the Caversham Wildlife Park. Neither one of them moved quickly. Maybe they had just finished breakfast and were ready for the next item on the day's agenda—snuggling up and dozing off for a mid-morning nap.

Discovering Downtown

A Unique Piece of History

In a country with few tangible pieces of early history, it is understandable why Aussies grab hold of all they can, even some that are obscure.

A set of 12 royal bells were cast and hung in London's St. Martin-in-the-Fields church during the 1300s. They rang on Sundays and for special occasions like honoring James Cook's setting sail to Australia in 1768.

About every 220 years, the bells are melted down and recast to improve their tone. The last time? A few decades before Cook's adventure. So, in the 1980s when they were slated to be recast again, a Perth businessman stepped in to save this unusual piece of memorabilia. He offered that this mineral-rich state would give the church enough copper and tin for a new set, in exchange for the 580 to 3,200-pound historic bells.

The Swan Bells, (the only royal set outside of England), are now housed in a specially designed glass spired building on Elizabeth Quay. Here volunteers continue to ring them every day to celebrate this country's history.

For Shoppers Only

In many parts of Europe, shopping is considered an integral part of daily life, not simply a chore to be endured. One way it's made more enjoyable and relaxing is to allow people to meander, have the chance to stop and chat with neighbors or admire store window displays. To accomplish this, cities set aside a part of town or dedicate avenues just for shoppers to stroll.

Perth is about as far as a place can be from Europe, but her city officials didn't forget their ancestral ties when they designed the downtown. Wisely, they connected the train station with a footbridge for passengers to easily enter the CBD's Murray and Hay Street pedestrian malls filled with specialty shops and restaurants.

Down one of Hay Street's alleyways is the popular London Court developed in the 1930s by mining magnate, Claude Albo de Bernales. This Englishman added a touch of home and whimsey to life in Oz by building a half-timbered Tudor style shopping arcade with a mechanical clock featuring jousting knights.

Splendid Esplanade

A city is much like a house. After a while, it feels lived in and in need of some sprucing up. However, the planning required to redevelop a city is much more extensive than remodeling a home.

In 2011, Perth officials decided the city needed to be reconnected with the river and they chose to revitalize the Esplanade Reserve. This was the ideal location because it was in the heart of the CBD, just steps away from the train station and the bell tower.

One of the first projects was to carve out a 2.7-hectare inlet for ferries and small boats to deliver passengers into the city center. Multiple plazas were created with two million cobblestones hand-laid in a gentle ripple design to mimic the river. A distinctive water park was installed representing the Noongar people's Dreaming story about how the Milky Way was created. Then the entire renovation was tied together with an eye-catching double arched footbridge which allows the public to feel a part of the water while observing it from above.

Artistic Ripples

Public art in the Land Down Under comes in all shapes and sizes. Like most forms of artistic expression, each piece is actually a sign of its time.

As part of the Esplanade Reserve's extensive redesign into a more vibrant mixed-use area, officials requested thematic sculptural concepts that integrated river life and the city. Western Australian-born artist Christian de Vietri won the $1.3 million competition with his six concentric arcs representing ripples in the Swan River. He named it *Spanda*, which is Sanskrit for to move a little. This is exactly what the artist hopes people will do—to move a little in and through the nine-story piece.

Spanda, or as the locals call it *The Paperclip*, is a true contemporary sculpture. Modern technology, materials and tools from 3-D modeling software to a fabrication plant that builds airplanes and spacecraft was required to create it. Then a crane lifted the individual arches into place to form the world's tallest, free-standing carbon fiber structure.

Loop Around Town

It's true. When most Perth area residents and visitors think of spending time outdoors, almost everyone's first thought is to head to one of the nearby beaches. No matter where you are, the Indian Ocean is only a few minutes away.

However, the city planners throughout the metro area understood that this region has much more to offer. So, they carefully designed the communities to be explored on foot and bicycle. And they thoughtfully incorporated the country's, "No worries, mate," philosophy into these projects by creating kilometers of pathways dedicated to just those on two wheels or two feet.

One of the most scenic paths is the 10-kilometer Swan River Loop which provides phenomenal city and river views from various angles. This route includes the lush South Perth Foreshore, the palm tree-lined Riverside Drive, as well as Elizabeth Quay and the Barrack Street Jetty. And for those too tired or lazy to travel the entire trail, there's always the ferry to take them back to the other side.

Perth's diverse ethnic groups have forever altered Australia—not just by how the country looks, but also how it thinks and even eats. Many people are beginning to take notice that this is no longer a sleepy backwater town on the other side of the country, particularly with its developing gastronomic reputation that rivals Melbourne.

One of the best ways to sample this area's burgeoning food scene is to attend the annual Twilight Hawkers Market. Every Friday evening from late spring through summer, hungry people can be seen following their noses to Forrest Place that's been filled with a tantalizing combination of aromas. This festive event is a street food aficionado's dream featuring dishes from Korea to Columbia to Holland. We noticed that some took a methodical approach to their taste-testing by savoring the delicacies from just one country. Others ventured from booth to booth, globetrotting with their taste buds. Either way it's a delightful introduction to this multi-cultural city.

Exploring the River

The Real Mythical Bird

The first literary mention of black swans was in a poem by the Roman satirist Juval in 82 A.D. Yet, his piece didn't express their beauty or fidelity, but rather how they were essentially a figment of one's imagination. For centuries, the black swan was a metaphor for something that didn't exist. It must have been a shock to the Dutch explorer, Willem de Vlamingh, and his crew when they landed on Australia's west coast in 1697 and actually saw black swans. Live specimens were later brought back to the continent and skeptical Europeans realized the impossible was real.

These elegant birds can be seen around Perth, especially floating down their namesake, the Swan River. They also grace flags, stamps, coins and many teams' jerseys. To us it seemed like the perfect combination of Aussie humor and hubris to explain why WA adopted the black swan as the state's symbol. This usage of the native bird is their way of saying, "We have been here all along. It just took you all a while to find us."

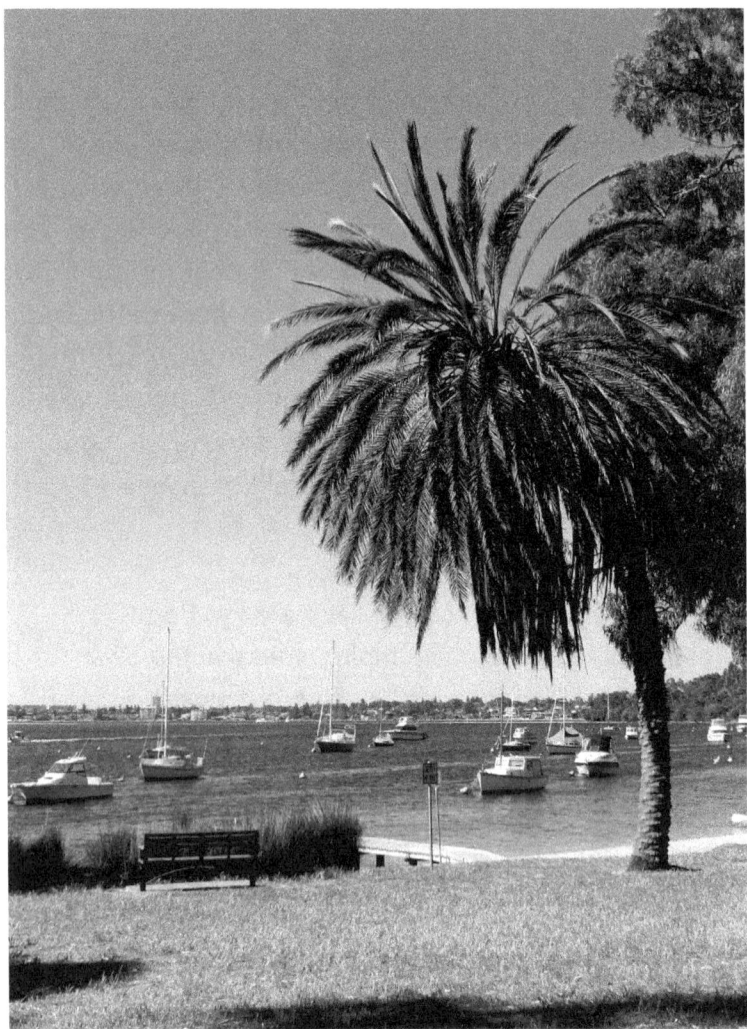

Everlasting

The palm tree lined esplanade featured tiny parks with postcard views of crystal blue water nestled against the white sandy coves. Sailboats and yachts of varying sizes and price tags completed the idyllic scene. From our vantage point it was easy to think this was the south of France as much as it was south Perth.

Our stroll along Bicton's picturesque two-kilometer walking trail wove between Blackwall Reach Parade and the Swan River. Before the Europeans arrived, this area was traditionally reserved for the Beeliar women and children of the Whadjuk Noongar people to use for camping, collecting plants and fishing. Furthermore, it was here during the Dreamtime that the Beeliar believe Junda, the Charnok spirit woman, picked up spirit children as she traveled through. They refer to the cliffs of Blackwall Reach as *Jenalup* or "the place where feet make a track" because they are thought to be her footprints. Junda may have left a lasting impact, but the only tracks we left were in the sand.

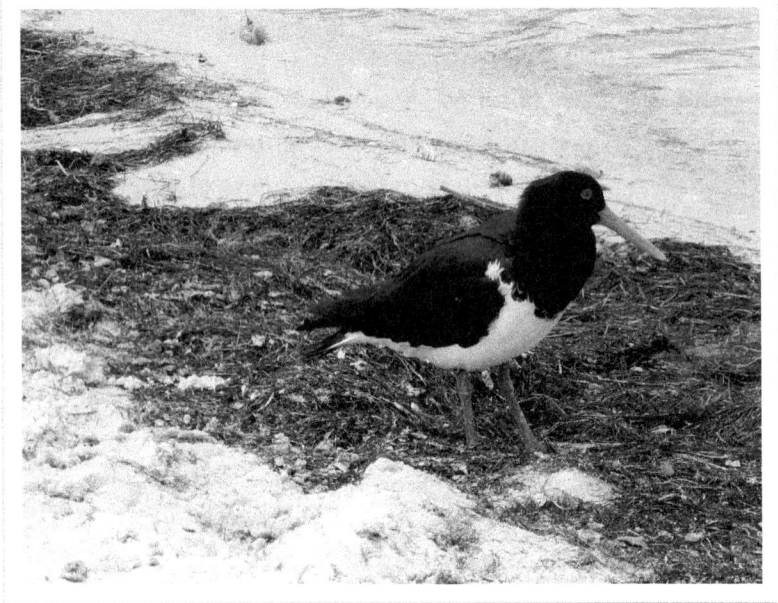

Just up the road from the sacred area of *Jenalup* is a thin white sandbar that stretches into the Swan River for over one kilometer near Point Walter. The Beeliar women and children used *Dyundalup* or "place of long flowing white hair" centuries ago. It was a pathway and meeting point to see their family group's men who lived on the opposite shore near Mosman Park.

This sandbar is now used by locals and visitors as a place to launch kayaks as well as to explore the river during low tide. It's also used as a nesting and feeding ground for several shorebirds including the Australian pied oystercatcher. This bird's long orange-red beak is specifically designed to pry open not oysters, but crabs, clams and mussels that he finds in or near the water's edge.

As we walked along the spit past this little guy, we found the colors of his body parts to be striking, particularly his fuchsia stockinged legs which stood out against the seaweed and sand. Beautiful, or as the Beeliar would say, *kwobardak.*

43

A Taste of Italy in Oz

Ever since the first colony was established, people from around the world have come to Australia for a new start. Yet, until the 1940s it remained a huge country with a tiny population. This fact worried government officials when 500,000 of the country's seven million citizens were shipped overseas to fight in WWII. They felt the homeland was left vulnerable to attack. Thus, after the war, Australians rolled out the welcome mat for new immigrants with the "populate or perish" program. British residents were asked first before the invitation was extended to other Europeans.

Over 280,000 Italians with bleak prospects at home decided to make the arduous journey. They brought with them some of life's essentials such as garlic and olive oil to spice up the food. Italian grape vines were imported to boost the fledgling Aussie wine industry into the world's fifth largest producer. And romantics will appreciate the ultimate Italian touch of a handcrafted gondola on the Swan. Ah, *la bella vita*.

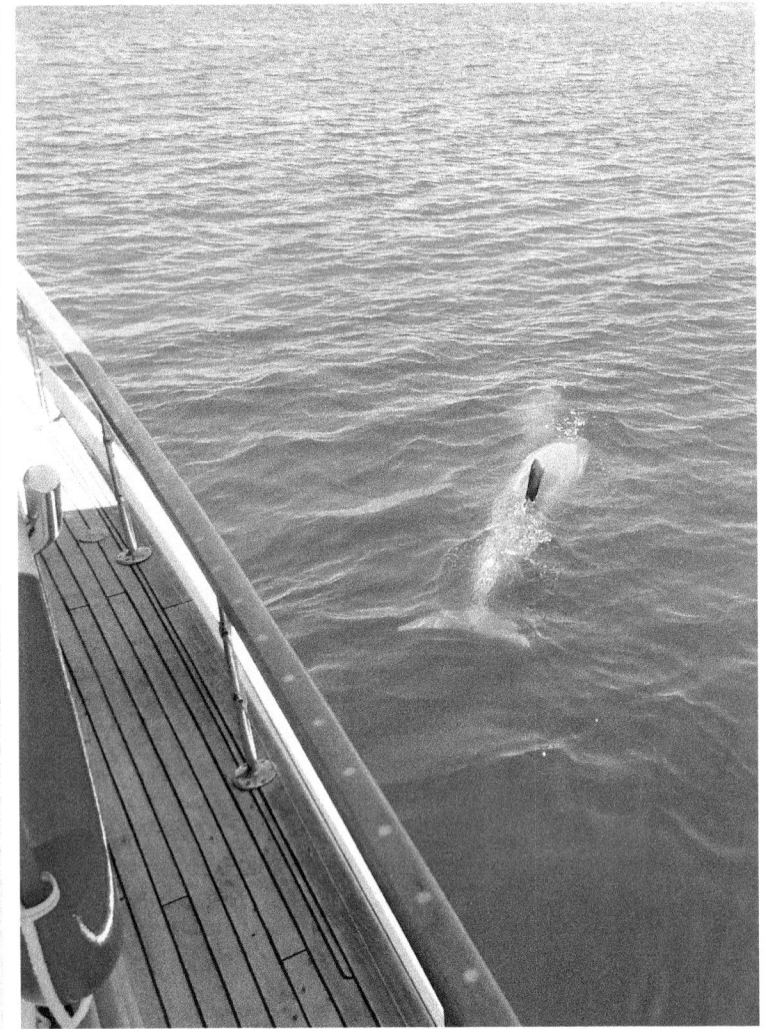

Dolphin Quest

The Swan River squiggles through Perth's metropolitan area. In some sections it's relatively narrow and shallow, like a stream. Other portions resemble a lake with bays and depths that invite scuba divers to explore. Perhaps one of its more unusual attributes is that it's an estuary. Water from the Indian Ocean flows into the Swan as do some of its creatures.

We'd heard that pods of bottlenose dolphins often swam in the river's deepest sections to feed. Though this helped limit the areas of where to look, timing was everything. And every time we walked along the foreshore, the closest thing we saw to dolphins surfacing were birds bobbing in the water.

One week before we left Perth, we spent a morning aboard an exquisite classic wooden boat. We were treated to a cruise part way up the river and tea in a quiet cove. Just as we were finishing our cake, a mother dolphin and her calf swam alongside the starboard side. Maybe they were enjoying for a mid-morning meal, too. Timing is everything.

Playing Outdoors in Oz

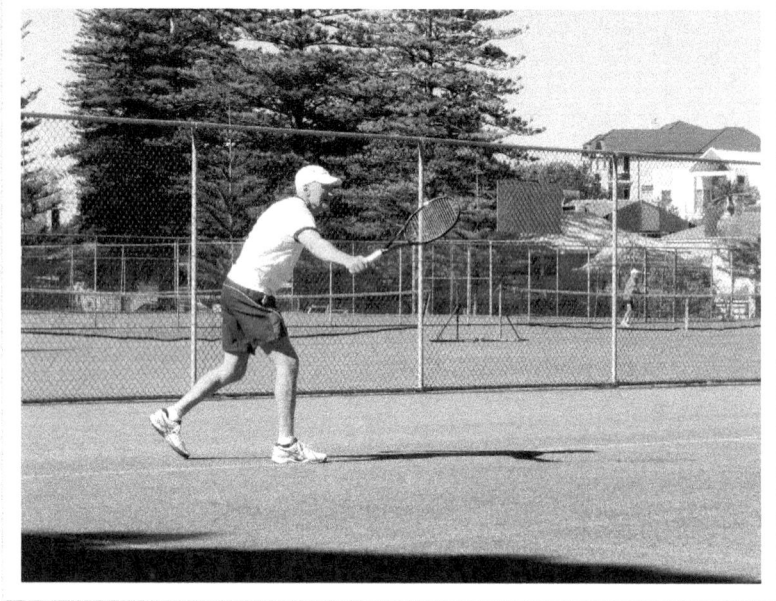

Tennis Anyone?

Historians dispute who first developed the sport of tennis. Some believe it can be attributed to 12th century monks. Others think that it wasn't until Henry VIII's day when racquets were used that tennis truly got its start. Nonetheless, most agree that it was Major Walter Wingfield who helped popularize the sport in England during the 1870s. He created a boxed set of equipment and encouraged people to play on lawns dedicated to croquet.

This natural surface is beautiful and very easy on the body. Yet, it requires an inordinate amount of time and patience to feed, mow and manicure. For this reason, almost all lawn tennis courts have been paved and turned into faster, more easily maintained, hard surfaces. That is, almost everywhere except Perth it seems. This metropolitan area boasts more grass courts than there are across the entire United States. Tennis purists may consider this city heaven because tradition lives on with so many of these rare, lush courts to play the sport they love.

Australia became an independent country in 1901. However, like Canada and New Zealand, Oz remains part of the British Commonwealth and some connections to Mother England are inextricably woven into everyday life.

Look on any flagpole. The Union Jack is a prominent design element in the upper left-hand corner of the Australian flag.

Listen to Aussies speak. Theirs is unquestionably a unique accent. Nevertheless, some words and phrasing have a British lilt that still lingers even centuries after the first immigrants landed here.

And on a sunny weekend, go to almost any city park. Amateur athletes are dressed in their white pants and team shirts to run, pitch and bat on cricket ovals. Colonists brought this English pastime to the Land Down Under and the Aussies are now considered some of the world's best players. Though we found cricket rules impossible to follow, it was easy to work up an appetite watching a game that featured food-oriented terms such as double-teapot, lollipop and pudding.

Sailing Sandgropers

Aussies are known for throwing in slang to add color to their speech. One example is nicknames. People here in Western Australia are often referred to as Sandgropers. While it's true that this insect is found in the state, the term seems as if it is an oxymoron. True sandgropers, or cylindrachetids, are subterranean burrowing creatures. Whereas, we found the human-kind around Perth eager to spend as much time as they possibly could enjoying the outdoors, particularly either in or on the water.

The combination of the area's Mediterranean climate and constant breeze off the Indian Ocean offers Perthies almost idyllic conditions for one of the country's favorite sports—sailing. Since the 1956 Melbourne Olympics, Aussies have brought home 27 sailing medals. Thus, people here are dedicated to start children out as young as seven years old to learn the ropes with the national Tackers program.

Every weekend we saw their mini sailboats on the waterways. Possibly one of them is a future Olympian?

Something for Everyone

A day at the beach. There's nothing more Aussie than that. And while each person's definition of the perfect day at the seashore may be different, Cottesloe is one of those exceptional places that offers something for everyone.

This stretch of pristine shoreline is located right between Perth and Fremantle. Cottesloe South is almost exclusively reserved for surfers and kiteboarders because it features higher waves and plenty of room for them to perform their stunts. Those who choose to don a mask and fins head north to Peter's Pool where the snorkeling is best. If someone just wants to splash in the water, swim or go boogie boarding, there's a magnificent area between the jetty and the striped buoy in front of the iconic pavilion. For everyone else, there are vast stretches of silky white sand by the water's edge or on lush green grass under the shade of the Norfolk Island Pines to play games or lie on a blanket.

Cottesloe captures Australia's spirit—having fun in the sun, surf and sand.

Dancing on the Water and Through the Air

Many people are thrilled just to get a simple kite in the air without crashing it into a tree. The exhilaration of kiteboarding—zipping across the water on a mini surfboard while holding onto a parachute-like kite— would be something they'd only dream of.

Western Australia generously offers two things that kiteboarders crave: plenty of wind and a coastline that seemingly goes on forever. Well, almost forever. The state has over 12,000 kilometers of shoreline beckoning those who want to give kiteboarding a try. (That's almost equivalent to all four UK countries' coasts combined.)

We joined a group of spectators to watch these giant kites dance along the shoreline. Several trick artists zoomed past us at 65 kilometers per hour as they flipped around doing Moby Dicks, Scarecrows, Tantrums and Fruit Loops. The crowd was in awe. We all knew if we ever attempted this extreme sport, we'd be lucky to do what the pros call "mowing the lawn," basically just standing up and holding on for dear life.

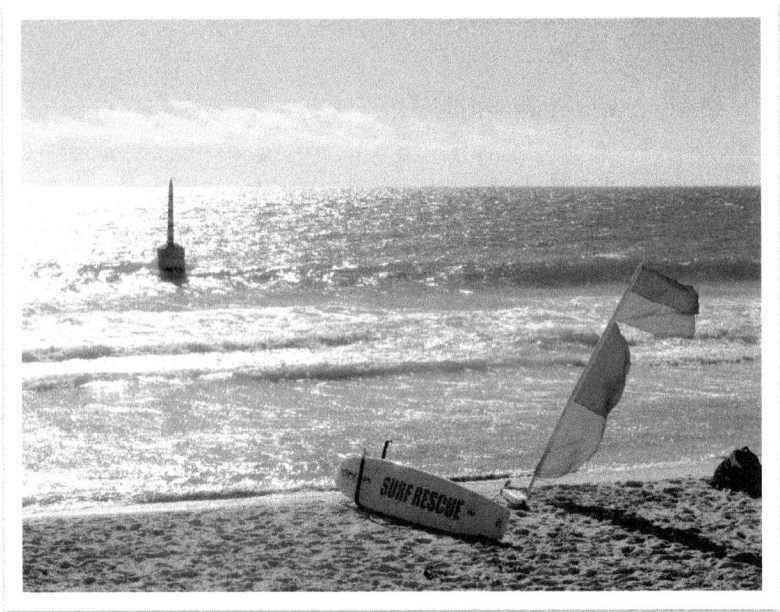

Playing It Safe

Western Australia's interior, like the Pilbara, has a unique, distinct beauty. Yet, it's undeniably dry and dusty. No wonder the majority of residents choose to live on or near the ocean. Who can resist a free, gargantuan pool so readily accessible?

Since most Aussies learn how to swim in school, if not younger, swimming is a major part of the country's culture and the number one sport nationwide. What many don't realize is that rip currents off Australia's coast pose a greater risk than shark attacks.

Enter the paid and volunteer surf lifesavers. These strong, courageous souls dash out into the water at the first sign of a swimmer in distress. They're also trained to read the currents and determine which parts of the beach offer the safest areas in which to swim. Each morning they plant their recognizable red and yellow flags between what they determine as the safe zone. Their hope is that beachgoers understand the flags aren't there for decoration but to help everyone have a good time.

Fremantle

Appreciating Aussie Art & Architecture

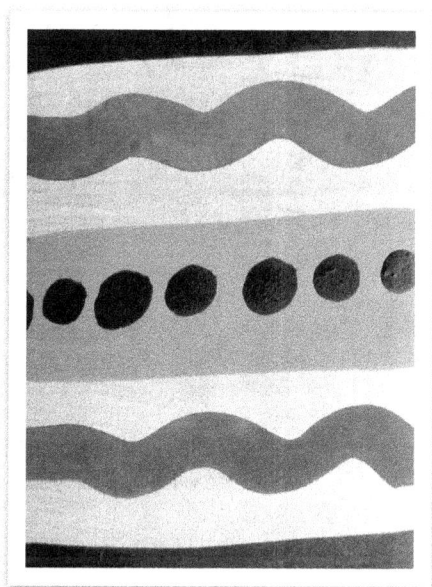

Relocating to Oz

Indigenous people had lived all across the Australian continent for millennia before Britain even knew about, let alone laid claim to it. Ships brought the first British settlers to the eastern states during the 1780s and the Swan River Colony was established in 1829.

Britain's biggest problem was now that they "owned" this land, not many really wanted to move here. Consequently, the colony struggled. Officials begged the crown to send them society's ne'er do wells as they'd done for Sydney, including petty thieves, counterfeiters and murderers. More than one-third of the 9,800 convicts were considered to be artisans and another third were laborers. By day they constructed the port and jetty, as well as the limestone buildings for a store, school and even their own prison.

In all, 43 ships transported convicts from 1850 to 1868 to serve out their terms here. Who knows how many stayed once they were freed? Those who made this their home maybe had a special pride in having helped build it.

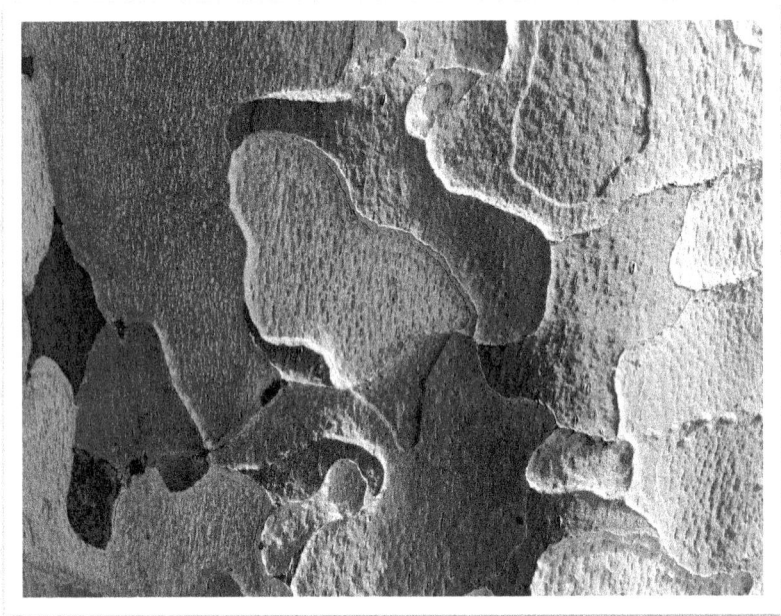

A City Filled With Art

Fremantle considers itself a community for artists. The government firmly believes that art plays an important role in community life and sets money aside to help support the arts.

There are the traditional forms of art such as theatre, dance and music that command attention whenever they happen to appear on stage. Audiences particularly relish the opportunity to watch these performances anytime they occur en plein air.

And then there are more subtle types of art that blend in with the scenery, just waiting for the passerby to notice. London plane trees line many of Fremantle's avenues. These heat and wind resistant plants provide more than just shade and a fantastic way to help keep the air clean. They also offer fanciful artwork. The bark of this one tree near the town's free shuttle bus stop reminded us of a collage adhered to a slender column. A few feet away on either side were similar, yet noticeably different presentations of this bas-relief design. What a spectacular collection.

If These Walls Could Talk

Some believe that the spirits of a building's past occupants often remain and color it forever. Perhaps that's why this edifice has been deemed the most haunted place in the southern hemisphere.

There could have been a curse left by the British convicts ordered to build the asylum in the 1860s or by the criminally insane patients, alcoholics and prostitutes who were inmates here. In 1909, the mentally ill were transferred to another facility and the building became a home for elderly women, a midwifery and later the American Army's WWII headquarters. Maybe the strife endured by those who have passed through here left an invisible, but indelible mark.

The Fremantle Arts Centre now occupies the limestone building. Several of its patrons have reported hearing voices, seeing apparitions, and even feeling sudden drops in temperature or the sensation of being kissed on the cheek. When we were there, all we saw was an avant-garde art exhibit. We could only wonder what the spirits thought of it.

Combining Passions

If there were a prize handed out to the country whose citizens strive to spend as much of their lives being outdoors, the Australians could win. And if they didn't earn first place, we bet they'd be in the top 10. However, as much as they like being outdoors, they're also an artistic bunch. Nine out of 10 Australians feels it's very important to have some creative skills and nearly everyone includes the arts in their life in one way or another.

Since the Land Down Under has a favorably warm climate, Australians are afforded numerous opportunities all year to combine their desire to be outside while enjoying the arts. In Fremantle, the Arts Centre offers a wide variety of outdoor arts programs from drawing workshops in the city square to concerts on their enormous lawn. One week it might be a marimba duo or possibly a folksinger serenading original ballads. We felt fortunate to take part in this aspect of Aussie life by savoring a gourmet picnic while listening to Vivaldi's *Four Seasons*.

Keeping an Ancient Culture Alive

Ever since the Europeans came to Australia, the Aboriginal people have worked hard to keep their 60,000-year-old culture a vibrant and vital part of life here. Fortunately, there are several opportunities available to gain insight into their venerable traditions. One of the best places is at the Walyalup Aboriginal Cultural Centre. This facility is open year-round and is just a short walk from the Fremantle train station. It offers a gallery and classroom with Noongar language, history and art lessons so others can become immersed in and appreciate aspects of this culture.

There's also an open invitation to the public to take part in the Wardanji Aboriginal Festival each October. This celebration purposefully coincides with the Fremantle Festival and is an excellent exhibition of colorful Noongar dances, songs and storytelling. These dynamic performances are enhanced by carefully designed costumes, makeup and lighting, while accompanied by the palpable reverberating tones of digeridoos.

Time Travel

Ever wonder what it'd be like to travel through time? A stroll through Fremantle's downtown may not transport you back to the late 1800s, but it's about as close as you'll get without Mr. Peabody's WABAC machine.

The city's home to an array of historical properties, including the world's best example of a 19th century port streetscape and more than 250 buildings on the state's Register of Heritage Places. These former bars, warehouses, factories, hotels and cottages were built during the gold rush era. They're extremely well preserved and offer a primer in Victorian architecture. Moreover, some continue to operate as they did over a century ago.

During the height of gold fever, the old National Bank of Australasia was converted into the National Hotel. It suffered a checkered past with the first owner shooting a councilman during a town meeting and enduring numerous fires. Now it boasts a swanky rooftop bar with an astounding view—a far cry from its gold mining days. How times do change.

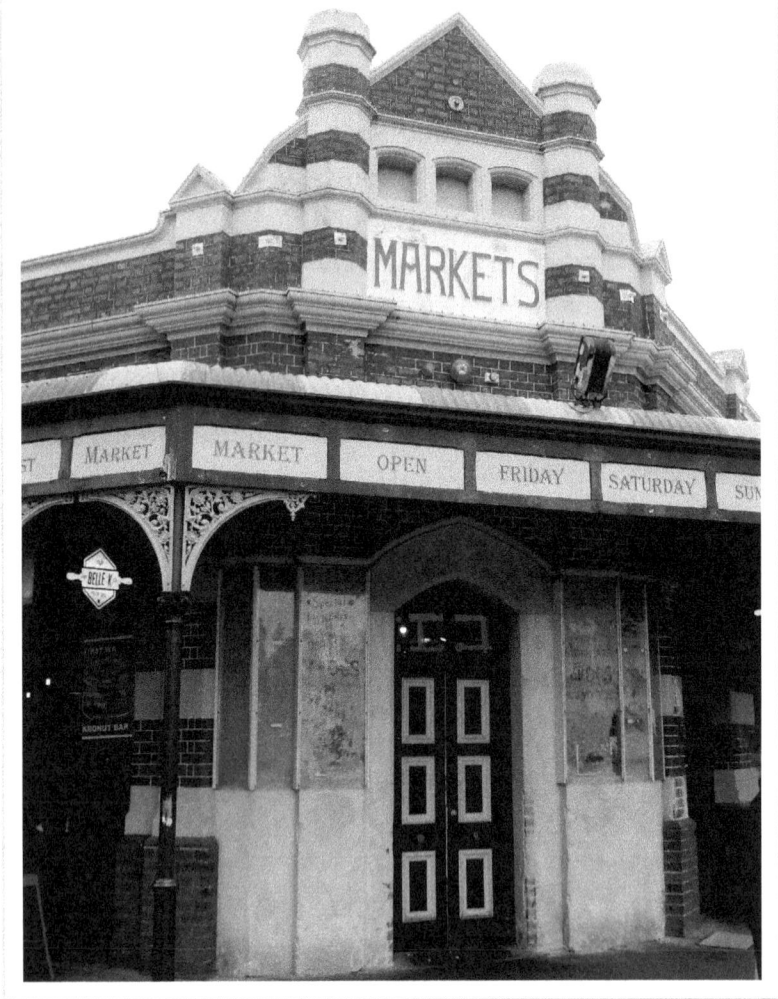

Market Potpourri

Another of the town's buildings that is listed on the Register of Heritage Places is the Fremantle Markets. This sprawling brick and limestone hall was built before the turn of the century after the Premier of WA, Sir John Forrest, laid the foundation stone. It is just one of the state's two surviving municipal market buildings and is one of only a handful in the country that still operates as it was originally intended.

The hall's focus has varied slightly throughout the decades. In the 1950s, it served mainly as a wholesale food and produce market. Then in the mid-1970s it underwent a complete restoration and now features over 150 permanent stalls with a hodgepodge of products and services jammed next to one another. Everything from Aboriginal art to gold-dusted cronuts to fashionable clothing to psychic readings is available within the narrow aisles. Locals and tourists alike enjoy meandering through this bustling market three days a week in search of an authentic taste of Australia.

The WA Style

Switzerland has chalets. Holland has canal houses. And America has Cape Cod-style homes. Though the overall shape and size of these houses may vary within a country, let alone a city block, specific design elements stand out that are recognizably distinct to the area.

There are one and two-story homes throughout this community that are referred to as Fremantle workers' cottages. When the English immigrants built these houses in the late 1800s, it appears as if they used several of their favorite architectural components to make this distant land feel like "home." Brick was a key building material for them here, just as it had been in England. They also cut blocks of the readily available limestone and incorporated these into their structures. Finally, the decorative touch of Victorian gingerbread trim provided an extra bit of flair.

The workers' cottage style may not be one that's copied in other parts of the world. Yet, it does have a charm all its own that adds character to the region.

Sampling Life in WA

The Port City

A port is a gateway into a country. What's imported and exported effects the area, how it can sustain itself and grow.

Fremantle's port is located adjacent to the Indian Ocean and has been the state's busiest harbor for over 150 years. Every hour of every day, $3 million AUD of trade is handled through this Swan River entrance and the auxiliary harbor 14 miles south.

Yet, this has been a gateway for more than just goods. From 1839 to 1890, over 26,000 souls came through here to make WA their home. Undoubtedly all of the state's new residents had concerns about what life in this new land would be like, especially the third of them who were convicts and came involuntarily.

Starting in 1898, Fremantle was the first port of entry for the majority of European passenger ships. Most immigrants continued on to the eastern seaports. However, the intrepid travelers who stayed in WA made a lasting impression on the state and their names are engraved on the 400 Welcome Walls near the port's entrance.

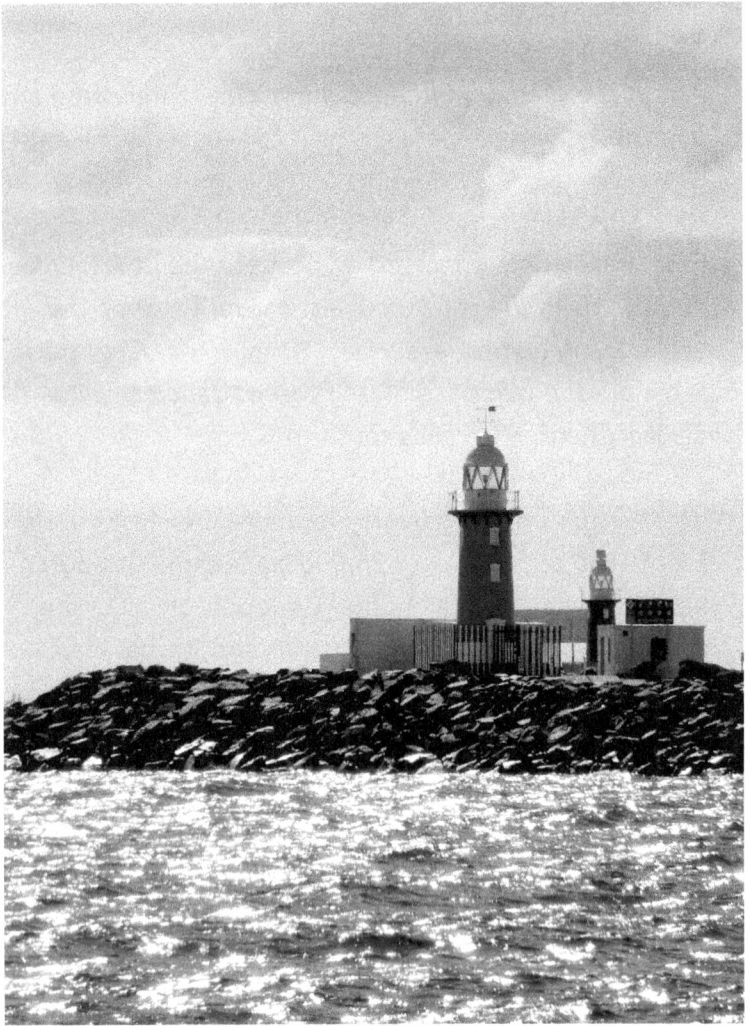

Beacons of History

Relics are everywhere. Some are hidden underground or underwater. Others are impossible to miss. But if they aren't labeled, one could pass them by, not recognizing their importance.

Sitting on opposite sides of Fremantle's Harbor are the North and South Mole Lighthouses. These twin cast-iron structures have been shining their beacons since 1903 to inform passing ships of their location. They're color coordinated and ready for Christmas year-round. The scarlet painted North Mole beams a red light while the South Mole is dressed in lime and flashes an intense emerald light.

One look at an area map and it's easy to understand how those living here could feel removed from the outside world. Yet, in 1942 after the tiny town of Broome was attacked, Fremantle became a hub for Allied submarines. WWII infrastructure still remains in front of the South Mole decades later from rusted pulleys to the yellow concrete observation post that was an anti-aircraft gun site. Relics right in broad daylight.

Adopting Traditions

Australia and America share two unusual bonds. Both were once part of the British Empire and, with the exception of the indigenous people, most of their citizens' ancestors immigrated by force or by choice. Consequently, their cultures became an amalgamation of traditions from multiple lands.

One ritual that was introduced to Oz by the Italian immigrants was the Blessing of the Fleet. This began in fishing communities along the Mediterranean coast centuries ago. Soon after WWII, Italian fishermen decided to celebrate it here as well in hopes that these extra prayers might help them remain safe and successful at sea.

An annual procession featuring two Madonna statues winds from Fremantle's basilica down to the shore. Hundreds then pile into boats with the decorated statues to tour the harbor and receive the priest's blessing before parading back to the church.

Who knows if this event gives the fishermen safer or more bountiful trips? At least it livens up the city with color and tradition.

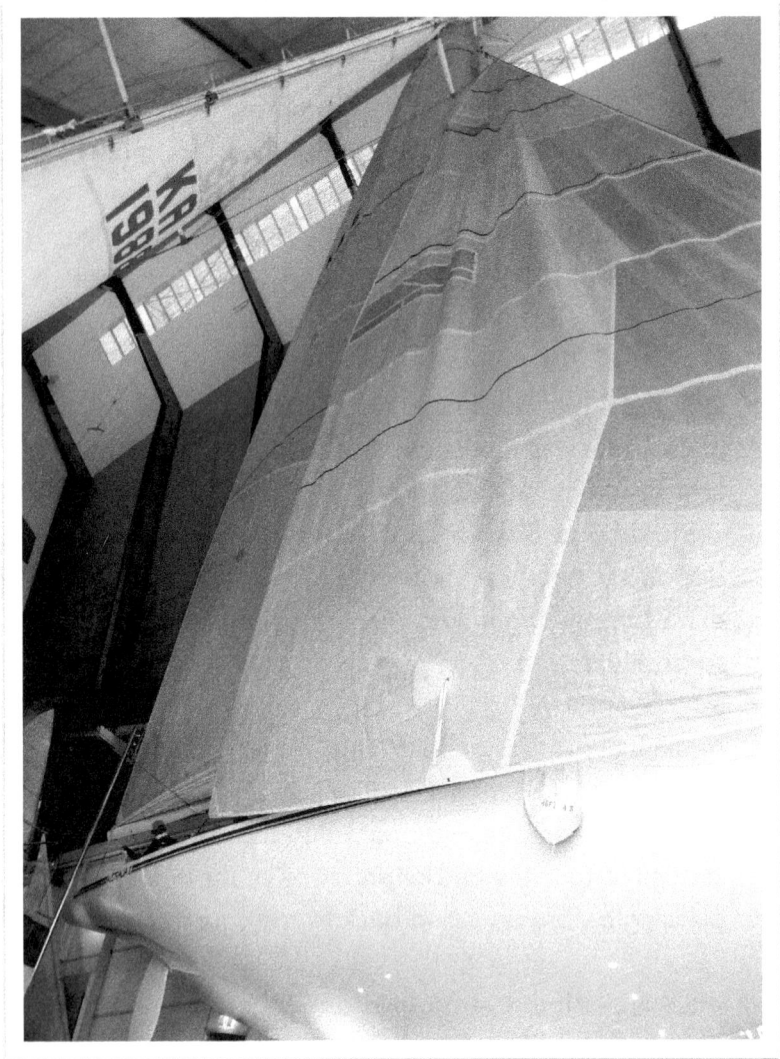

The Pride and Joy of Oz

To Australians it's a shrine that many venture cross-country to admire. To Americans it's a reminder that everyone is human.

John Bertrand and his crew traveled to Newport, Rhode Island in the autumn of 1983 to do the unthinkable. They challenged the United States in this sleek yacht, Australia II, to win the America's Cup. After the first four races, the US team needed one more victory to maintain the longest winning streak in sports. Yet, the determined Aussies proceeded to win the next three races and for the first time in 132 years, the coveted Auld Mug left the US.

Australia had bragging rights for over three years until a defense was set to take place in Fremantle. The town spent millions to undergo major renovations, prepare itself for the world's spotlight and throw a five-month long party. Sadly, the Aussies lost the best of seven series, four to zero. Nonetheless, this yacht that changed sporting history will forever be a point of pride in Fremantle's Western Australian Museum.

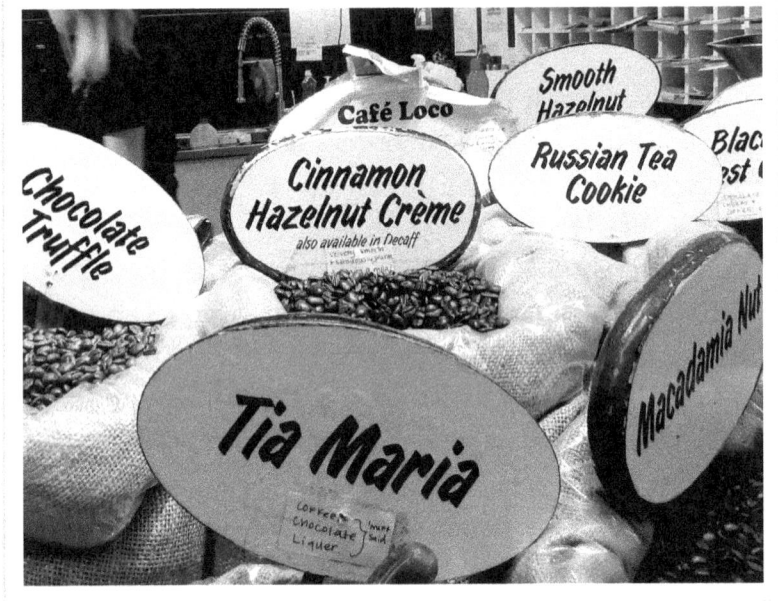

Chocolate Truffle

Café Loco

Cinnamon Hazelnut Crème
also available in Decaff

Smooth Hazelnut

Russian Tea Cookie

Blac
est

Macadamia Nut

Tia Maria

coffee
Chocolate
Liquer

Cafés and Cuppas

This country's coffee culture roots can best be traced back to the Italians who first immigrated to Oz during the gold rushes of the 1850s and 1890s. These roots grew deeper after WWII when neighborhood cafés sprang up everywhere. And despite marketing efforts by chains like Starbucks, Aussies prefer to have a *chinwag* (chat) and a *cuppa* (hot drink) with their friends at home or a locally owned café. South Terrace, affectionately referred to as the Cappuccino Strip, is unquestionably one of the state's best spots to experience this part of the culture.

We discovered that Australians are serious not only about where they drink their coffee, but also what they drink. One in three coffees prepared in Western Oz is a concoction called the flat white. This espresso-based drink topped with milk was first developed in Australia during the mid-1980s and is considered to be less frothy than a latte.

No matter how the coffee is served or where, this is an integral part of Aussie life to be savored.

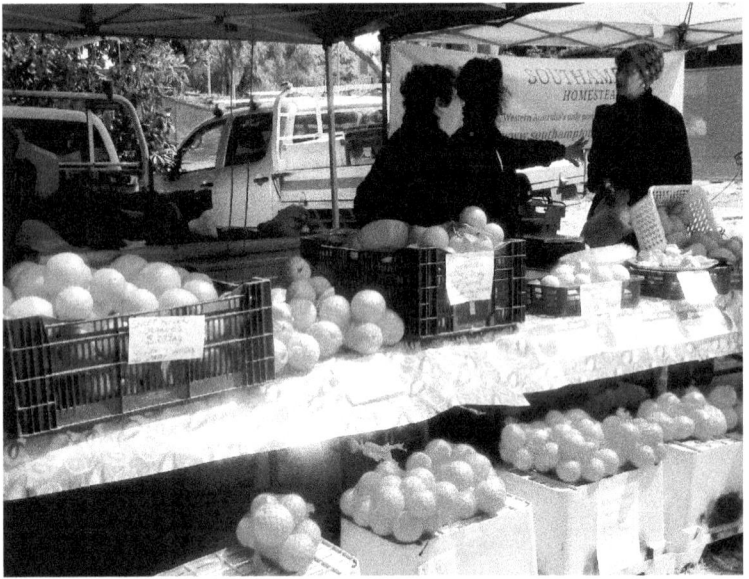

Social Shopping

Every weekend there are dozens of farmers' markets throughout the Perth area. These are popular meeting places where people can buy fresh produce and baked goods, as well as sample regional wines or exotic foods. One such example is the Sunday market in Beaconsfield that's held in a schoolyard. Here families shop, then sit on the lawn while sharing a cuppa and some of the week's stories.

Because the market's vendors tend to be the same week and after week, they too play a significant role in this neighborhood scene. Two of our favorites were the gregarious Orange Ladies who sold fresh oranges and lemons from their family's orchard south of Fremantle. They were sisters-in-law who were quick to offer an orange slice and a few jokes. We admired how they skillfully tended to their customers while continually hauling heavy crates and bags of fruit from their truck into their makeshift store.

Farmers' markets aren't just for locals. They're where everyone can be a local, even for just an hour.

On the Lookout

Some travelers say they'd love to visit Australia but can't bring themselves to buying a ticket. Their trepidation isn't due to cost or the long flight, but fear of the country's poisonous critters including jellyfish, spiders and snakes.

Oz does have more than its share with 66 creatures that can cause serious harm. However, it's the tourist haven of Mexico that actually tops the list with 80. That may be of little comfort since Australia has the distinction of being home to 14 out of the world's 15 most venomous snakes. And signs like this one on the pathway near South Beach would cause almost everyone to think twice.

Yet, here are some facts to put those with ophiophobia more at ease. About 90 percent of snakes in the country can't kill humans or even cause severe illness. Furthermore, snakes tend to avoid humans and rarely attack unless they feel threatened. A quick look around and yielding the right of way is usually all it takes to prevent a bad encounter with a slithering serpent.

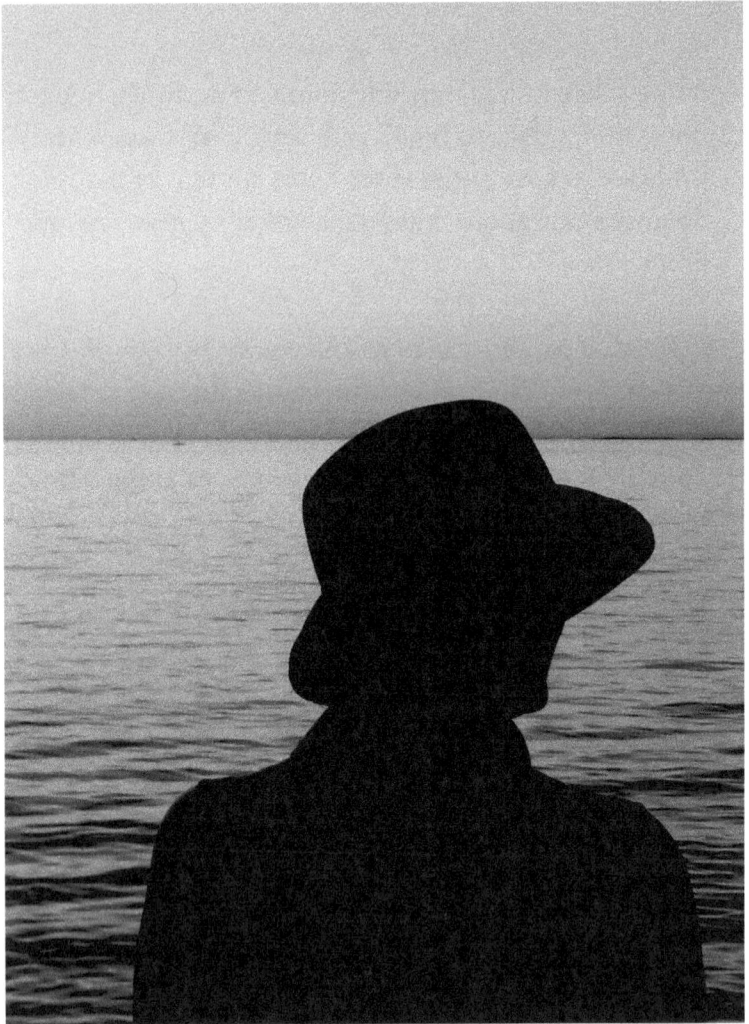

Savoring the Sunset at South Beach

We strolled down to South Beach. It was a luscious evening with only a hint of a breeze. Nights like this are just one reason why people live here and don't mind that it's one of the world's best kept secrets.

South Beach is a city park that offers all of the essentials for Aussie outdoor living. There's a large lawn with the requisite barbies where several families can grill their dinner. A designated off-leash area is a popular spot for man's best friends to romp. And of course, there's easy access to the white sand beach right next to the ocean.

Our walk took us along the groyne, a jetty-like structure of boulders and compacted sand. We passed by dozens of elegant sailboats bobbing in the harbor and made our way to the point. There we had a superb view of the Ferris wheel all aglow in Esplanade Park. Then we turned to watch South Beach's premier attraction. What a marvelous way to say goodnight with a pastel sky show over the Indian Ocean while dreaming of sailing off into the sunset.

Just Outside of Town

Admiring Nature in
John Forrest National Park

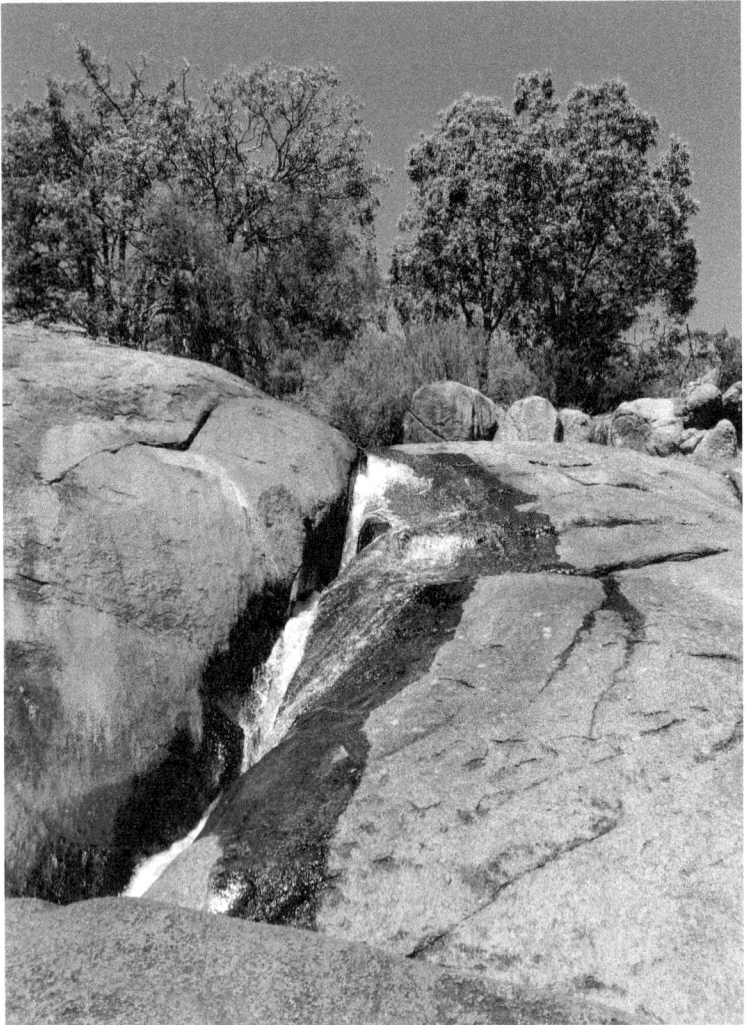

Nearby Wilderness

Perth may be a huge city, yet one doesn't have the feeling of being trapped like in other metropolises. Maybe this is because there are the vast playgrounds of the Swan River and Indian Ocean running right through and alongside her. On top of this, there are four national parks within a 50-kilometer drive from town.

The closest of these is WA's first national park and the second in the entire country. It's named after the state's first premier, John Forrest, and offers visitors a wide array of sites along its trails.

Our hike took us past a jumble of boulders, some as large as smart cars. In among the stones were patches of late-blooming wildflowers ranging in color from amethyst to pale amber. The trail led us by smooth massive rock slabs that reminded us of a thick coat of peanut butter generously spread down the hillside. Our favorite parts of the journey were the streams that sliced through narrow ravines. The cool water was refreshing, like an oasis under the blazing Australian sun.

Three in the Bush

National parks offer a little bit of everything to visitors. And whether someone's a camper or a day-tripper, one can fill up his or her senses with nature.

The first thing we noticed about this 26.7 square kilometer refuge was the enticing mint, pine and honey aroma of the bush that had been seemingly baked in the sun. We were also struck by the textures and colors of the various trees and rocks set against the bright blue sky.

A trio of red-tailed black cockatoos caught our attention as they flitted above from tree to tree. They kindly rested long enough on the upper branches of this eucalyptus for us to examine them. The male with his crimson namesake tail feathers was very camera shy. His two female companions, on the other hand, proudly showed off their head and shoulder plumage decorated with speckles, plus contrasting yellow and orange tail feathers. A minute later they were off again. Our guess was they were on their way to a party. These birds were definitely native Australians.

Sitting in the Ol' Gum Tree

The kookaburra looked down at us from his perch with a comical look. It was impossible not to think about the song we'd heard as children and wonder how much of it was true.

We discovered that about the only part that's accurate is the first line. This little guy and other kookaburras do live in eucalyptus forests which are often referred to as gum trees. Yet, though he's called a kingfisher, he's not very regal. One reason is because his laugh-like call is reminiscent of old *Tarzan* movies and sounds like that of a court jester than the king.

The lyricist also took liberties with the kookaburras' diet. They don't eat any gumdrops, whether from tree sap or a candy store. Mice, lizards and snakes top their menu. In fact, at the turn of the 20th century, kookaburras were introduced here from their native eastern Oz habitat to reduce the snake population.

And as for counting monkeys in the forest, Australia has none outside of zoos. This verse, like most of the song, was written just for fun.

We couldn't help but smile.

A hike through this park was the ideal getaway. It allowed us to explore the bush and see plants we'd never seen before. Some of them were so whimsical that we felt as if we were walking through the pages of a Dr. Seuss book.

This curious-looking species of grass trees is just one of 18,000 kinds that is exclusively found in Australia. They reminded us of humongous green sea urchins plopped onto stubby blackened trunks of varying shapes. Furthermore, their singular flowers are phantasmagorical because they grow to be well over nine feet tall and resemble a giant's spear.

We were surprised to learn that even though this grove of trees is relatively short, their size is no indication of their age. Chances are they started growing here well before the first European sailors landed on Western Australia's shores in 1606.

What could be better? A botany and history lesson wrapped into one walk through a quirky forest that encouraged us to let our imaginations run wild.

Bushwalking in
Walyunga National Park

Water Symphony

Our seats were waiting for us. We had our pick of boulders scattered on the bank to sit and watch the river's show. It first bounced down Syd's Rapids, then zig-zagged past, lurching over rocks in some sections or forming deep pools near the far edges. As we closed our eyes we could hear and feel the water's percussive dynamics. It moved from a rushing roar before carefully following the composer's cue with a steady decrescendo to a soft trickle.

These sites and sounds in the Walyunga National Park impressed us for two reasons. It was a respite from the city, but moreover it was fascinating to see this part of the Swan River. We enjoyed the different view with just eucalyptus trees towering over its shore rather than houses and office buildings. Could this really be the same body of water?

The Noongar people had used the area as a meeting place and campsite for about 6,000 years. A rough translation of the setting's name is happy place. What an appropriate moniker for such a lovely spot.

The Essence of the Bush

Before we ventured into this park, we asked some locals to define what "the bush" is. Surprisingly, they told us that it doesn't have the same look and feel for everyone. Nevertheless, Aussies have a special connection with the bush. One that's almost visceral.

Though no one describes it the same, we discovered there are common, essential elements to the bush. Most believe it's a woodsy area. Some indicate there are grassy spots. Others say there are none. But most everyone agrees that it contains low-growing bushes and the ubiquitous eucalyptus trees. Another common denominator is that the bush is relatively undeveloped. It may be a park that's been left wild within a city. Yet, more than likely it's like this spot in one of the state's wide-open spaces where no people live.

For us, the essence of the bush was that it was a place where we could be in nature and a part of it. This was where the outside world didn't intrude, and we could simply listen to the birds, the water and the wind.

Cozy Joyride

We sauntered back toward our car after spending most of the day in the park. Since the pathway was fairly straight and flat, we didn't have to pay much attention to where we were going. The well-maintained trail allowed us to spend more time admiring the meadow of wildflowers and relishing the dappled shade of the gum trees rather than watching out for obstacles.

Then off to our right something caught our eye that made us stop in our tracks. Two adult kangaroos stood in a clearing while they munched their afternoon snack of various grasses. When the smaller one wandered behind a tall shrub, we stared more closely at the bigger animal who kept on eating. She was larger for a reason. There was a tiny head with huge ears poking out from her pouch. Her joey was about eight months old and seemed rather curious about the world. However, his curiosity didn't seem to outweigh his preference for relaxing and enjoying the warm ride. He soon decided the adventure could wait and disappeared inside.

Day-tripping to Rotto

Island Secrets

Places, like people, have secrets. To discover them could require unearthing a cache or peeling back layers of wallpaper to find treasures former owners left behind. Other times there might be a trove of information buried in dusty archives.

Rotto (Rottnest) is a relatively small island with a past that tells two very different stories. For most, it has been a recreational haven with dozens of sugar white beaches, perfect for fishing, snorkeling, diving and just having fun.

Yet, few are aware of the island's dark history. These 19 square kilometers served as a prison for almost a century, holding indigenous prisoners in deplorable conditions and often chained together by their necks. It also was an internment camp during WWI and WWII for immigrants whose only "crime" was that their former home country was at war with Australia.

Some believe that it's best to leave the past in the past. However, learning the history of a place can help provide a better understanding and appreciation of it.

Hollywood's filled with actors. Yet, few receive much acclaim or time in the spotlight. The same is true for most of the unusual creatures indigenous only to Australia. Kangaroos and koalas are Oz's most famous duo. These two marsupials have been adopted as the country's national mascots and brand ambassadors. However, there are others exclusive to the Land Down Under that are relative unknowns.

Quokkas receive minimal limelight and will never be household names. One reason is because they're mainly nocturnal. On top of this, they're essentially hidden from the rest of the world, living only in the southwestern corner of Western Australia.

We spotted this little guy in a thicket on the island. He's a member of a 10,000+ colony. It's the largest in the world, but we only saw nine. His short, blocky build reminded us of his wombat cousin, but he hopped around like a miniature wallaby. He kindly interrupted his afternoon walk to pose for us, almost as if to say, "I'm ready for my close-up."

A Fine Feathered Friend

Ornithologists have determined that there are about 9,000 to 10,000 species of birds on Earth, of which roughly five percent (or 550) live in Western Australia. Some of these are commonly found on several other continents such as the raven or barn owl, while a handful are unique to Oceania.

The Australian Pelicans' habitat extends throughout the continent as far east as Fiji and north to New Guinea. Yet, the majority of them just fly around their namesake country. They resemble their worldly cousins in many respects, but with one important distinction. These Aussies have the largest bill of any living bird measuring 188 centimeters. Their extraordinary mouths serve as fishing nets that can scoop up 13 liters of water, plus dinner.

We found this pelican sunning himself near Geordie Bay. He patiently posed for a few photos in which he appeared to be almost smiling. Then he slowly opened his beak wider and wider, signaling that he had grown tired of us. Just one more use for his giant bill.

Watching the Parade Go By

The Fremantle ferry let us off at the main harbor. While we didn't have the place to ourselves, all of the passengers disappeared from the dock so quickly that it felt as if we were on a semi-private island.

Many hurriedly set out on the 22 kilometers of roadway dedicated to bikes (and the island's two motorized busses). We could have joined them, but we decided to explore this car-free island on foot. It was a delicious day, the kind that encouraged us to just mosey barefoot along the shore. And oh, what a shoreline it was. Crystal clear water with little coves, idyllic for swimming or just dabbling our toes in.

At the postcard-like setting of Little Parakeet Bay we spread out our towels on the snow-white sand to watch the parade. First, several sailboats gracefully waltzed by on the turquoise water. Next came a large flock of pelicans who flew in a staggered formation. However, our favorite was the humpback whale who performed three aerial pirouettes. A perfect ending to a perfect day.

Headed North

Roaming the Backroads

Be Careful What You Wish For

The hamlet of Toodyay lies an hour's drive north of Perth and features 36 colonial buildings that range from 100 to 150 years old. Almost ancient by Australian construction standards. Well-preserved Aussie architecture aside, the story behind who helped build some of them is unusual.

Within the first year after the Swan River Colony requested British convicts, four ships arrived, one sooner than anticipated and another that was a surprise. The fledging government was overwhelmed, lacking enough resources to feed and house all of the prisoners now in their charge. So, the governor granted some lucky souls Tickets to Leave. In essence they were given automatic paroles for time served. The terms of their release required them to stay and work within the area.

Initially 40 former convicts were chosen to go to Toodyay to assist in the construction of buildings and roads. They were free, however paid a steep price by enduring rough conditions in a backwoods place, thousands of miles from home.

Spring's Curtain Call

Every year, from late winter to early spring, one of nature's best shows takes place across the state. People mark their calendars for the free floral extravaganza to blanket the region in vivid gold, purple, blue, white and pink blossoms.

By the time we arrived, the flowers were wrapping up their multi-month performance. We may have missed the star attraction, but we had the chance to experience something different that made us appreciate this place even more.

A ten-minute walk away from our car was all it took to prove to us just how formidable a place the Australian bush is. In short, it's hot. Very hot. And this was only the first week of October.

We couldn't help but be impressed by how these fragile flowers were blooming despite the unforgiving conditions. The last rains may have ended weeks earlier, yet these vibrant dots of life were flourishing in this parched soil. Our guess was that they wouldn't last much more than a day or two. We were glad to be there for their curtain call.

Away From It All

Up and down the coast are dots on the map, each with only a handful of stop signs. These are the towns where most wouldn't think to pull over and explore unless they knew someone or had a flat tire. And yet, they can offer some of the most memorable experiences.

One such place is Wedge, named for the triangular patch of land on which it sits, surrounded by the Wanagarren Natural Reserve. The town itself may not appear to be anything special with its dozens of beach shacks. Yet, it only took one look at this ocean view to know the long drive from Perth had been worthwhile. The turquoise, cobalt, and sapphire water contrasted with the ivory sand was one of the most striking beach views we've ever seen.

It's true Wedge doesn't have much in the way of fine dining, except all of the fresh seafood ready to be caught straight from the ocean. And there isn't any real nightlife, except all of the stars in the Southern sky you can count while telling stories by a campfire. Memories for the making.

Sci-fi Desert

Some places look as if they belong somewhere else in the solar system, other than Earth. The Pinnacles in the Nambung National Park is one such spot. Thousands of limestone formations seem to have randomly popped out of the golden desert. Many look like knee-high stumps. Others appear to be intricately etched avant-garde sculptures with razor-sharp tips.

As we wandered through the surreal landscape, we half-expected Captain Kirk and his away team to beam down, ready to greet whatever alien species lived there. Though we saw no signs of life, there are over 100 types of birds, two types of kangaroos and even 15 different reptiles that live in this park.

Had the Enterprise's science officers transported down to this bizarre surface, they would have been as baffled as we were trying to determine how these outcroppings had formed. Geologists have put forth three theories, yet none are able to settle on a definitive reason. Just one more thing that adds to this place's uniqueness and mystery.

Windswept Reminders

There was a time when the area around Greenough was thriving. English settlers had been enticed to travel to the other end of the Earth for a better life. Affordable 20 and 30-acre parcels of land were made available to them to establish small wheat farms. Consequently, a community of over 1,000 began to flourish here 24 kilometers south of Geraldton. It was replete with a mill, store, hotel, several churches and schools. Yet, nature had other plans. A terrible cyclone struck the region in 1872 and was followed by a devastating flood in 1888. When gold was discovered a few years later in Coolgardie, the lure of "quicker" fortunes all but decimated the community.

What remains now are only a handful of buildings, most of which belong to the National Trust of Australia. Perhaps one of the most poignant reminders of the settlers' abandoned dreams is a one room school house. Vacant. It stands alone in a field accompanied only by the windswept gum trees reaching over to gently touch the roof.

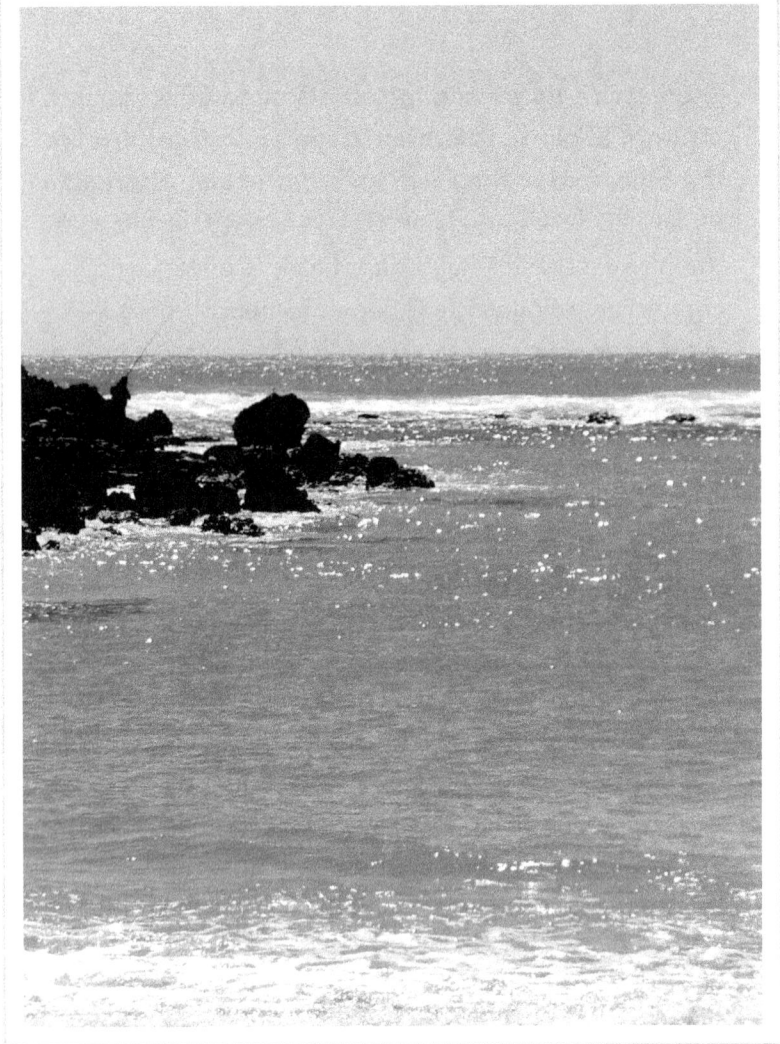

Western Australia is the perfect antidote to feeling claustrophobic or stressed. There's a sense of calm here that's pervasive.

This tranquility may be attributed to the state's low population or the fact that it's not overrun with tourists. Another reason could be that the Aboriginal people's way of life encourages a connection to all that's around them to help create an inner peace. Their enduring culture has in effect permeated the land, the air and the water.

We found this serenity to be especially prevalent along the Coral Coast, an area punctuated with small laid-back towns. The white sand and rocky shoreline serve as one long welcome mat inviting anyone to come and relax.

This fisherman was spotted near Geraldton, happy to be next to the Indian Ocean with his pole. The graceful, deliberate rhythm to how he cast his line into the water resembled a Tai Chi master. He exuded the region's Zen-like attitude, not caring whether he caught anything, content just to be there in that moment.

Pink Lady

It'd be easy to think that this picture was altered in Photoshop®. It wasn't. Nor was it the result of a giant April Fool's Day joke of spilling 100 dump trucks filled with food coloring. The truth is, there are several lakes around the world that are naturally bubblegum pink. Some are in Africa. A few can be found in Europe. Yet, Australia boasts the majority of these unusual beauties.

One of the most accessible pink lakes is in the fishing community of Port Gregory. Hutt Lagoon lies just below sea level with only a sliver of land between it and the Indian Ocean. Consequently, salty underground springs trickle into the lake and provide the ideal conditions for the carotenoid-producing algae *Dunaliella salina*. All that is needed is some sunlight (of which this part of Western Australia has in abundance) for this algae to produce beta-carotene, the same reddish pigment found in carrots. There's no need to worry though, no matter how much beta-carotene you consume, you'll never turn pink.

Traveling Around the Kalbarri

Grand Dame

Canyons and gorges are nature's sculptures that are essentially constant works in progress. These deep valleys have teams of finicky artists forever chipping away at them, never satisfied to call the pieces complete. There's the river that snakes along the foundation carving curves and straight lines as it pleases. Add to this the wind, rain and varying temperatures that chisel away at the walls, plus significant contributions made by the tectonic plates.

In many ways, the Kalbarri National Park's Murchison Gorge reminded us of the Grand Canyon. It was an eye-catching geologic formation, in the middle of nowhere and was quite hot, even on a spring morning.

However, some may claim that with a depth of only a fraction of its American cousin, the Australian gorge is far less impressive. We disagree. While the Grand Canyon is truly extraordinary, the Murchison Gorge is also deserving of the spotlight, if for no other reason than she's been in Mother Nature's gallery 330 million years longer.

Rocky Road

WA is filled with parks that offer a variety of day hikes: in the bush near streams, along the coast and even through deserts. Most of these places feature paths that are easy to traverse because they follow the shoreline or are well-defined, well-maintained routes. However, there's at least one path in the Kalbarri National Park that seems to almost dare hikers to explore. We took the challenge because we had most of the essentials— sturdy boots, hats, sunscreen and water. Sadly, we'd forgotten the nets for our hats to keep away the pesky flies. Big mistake.

The track led us through ancient gullies and along towering sandstone walls down into the Murchison Gorge. It wasn't arduous, rather more of an adventure negotiating staircases of boulders. Along the way, we appreciated the tenacity of the trees and plants that had managed to take root in the rock crevices and survive the arid conditions. After a break down on the river bank, we clambered up and over the rocks again back to our car.

Captivating. That's the best way to describe the cliffs of Kalbarri's Castle Cove. This is truly one of Australia's most stunning scenes. Perhaps it's the colors. They're arresting. We admired the varying shades of turquoise waters with a foamy white line squiggling along the shore, juxtaposed against the perfectly stacked layers of cream, red and brown sandstone. Maybe because it was around lunchtime and we were hungry, but the rocks reminded us of a giant puffed pastry on a humongous blue plate.

What added to this spot's beauty was her age. She looked exceptional for something standing over 300 million years. Yes. There were obvious cracks and wrinkles, yet this is what made her extraordinary. The cliffs' surface was similar to an elder's face that proudly showed the lines caused by everyday life. If only we could hear the stories that this ancient one has witnessed from when the dinosaurs roamed above to the explorers whose ships slammed into her base to life now in the 21st century.

Kalbarri is a small town with less than 1,600 residents. Nevertheless, it has several restaurants. Most of which probably serve good, maybe even great food. Yet, this is one of those places with such fascinating scenery that we didn't want to take the time to eat inside. Dining alfresco in one of the numerous parks seemed a far better choice.

We chose a spot which turned out to be a haven for surfers. What could be better—free entertainment while we ate overlooking the area's 400-million-year-old Tumblagooda Sandstone formations juxtaposed with the Indian Ocean?

Some surfers wore full wetsuits. Others were in colorful boardies (board shorts). Regardless of their attire, all were after the same thing—the chance to carve through a continuous curling wave. In some ways they reminded us of bull riders. They pitted their balance and strength against the unpredictability of a natural, powerful force. Many wiped out. Those who managed even a few second ride received our applause and admiration.

Colorful Coastal Cliffs

Britain's White Cliffs of Dover are well known for their beauty. When we visited them, we were struck by how the 350-foot limestone bluffs appeared to be plastered in a near perfect accordion pattern. And if we'd had a high-powered telescope, we possibly could've seen the city of Calais, France across the English Channel.

Not so famous, but equally as dramatic, are the cliffs of Pot Alley near Kalbarri. These ancient rocks are composed of the ubiquitous red sandstone found throughout much of Western Australia. Here the master builder's tool of choice seems to have been a huge roller rather than the trowel he used in Dover. First he created wafer-thin sheets and then carefully stacked them one on top of another like pyramids.

Time and erosion have significantly worn away the apexes of Pot Alley's bluffs. Nevertheless, the scene's age and magnificence were humbling, as was its remote location thousands of miles from Antarctica to the south, Indonesia to the north and South Africa due west.

A Few Hours South

Sightseeing Close By

Treasure Hunt

It took a bit of time and some luck, but we found them.

There are about 1,200 fairy penguins who call Penguin
Island home. So, it seemed reasonable to think we'd
spot at least a dozen of the irresistible creatures
waddling around this 31-acre park near Rockingham.
Yet, these little guys are experts at playing hide-and-
seek. When they aren't in the water swimming or
fishing, they're staying cool in their cave-like nests.

The island's Discovery Centre provides information and
the chance to view a handful of fairy penguins up close
who were abandoned as chicks or recovering from
injuries. While they are entertaining, it's not as
rewarding watching captive birds frolic in an indoor
wading pool as it is to encounter them in nature.

We walked around much of the island. There were no
wild penguins to be seen. Then down near the shore we
turned toward a rocky overhang. Nestled in the crevice
about 15 meters away was a penguin family. That
sighting was like finding a treasure—fleeting yet lasting.

166

Penguin Island's Other Residents

This bird refuge, just a stone's throw from the mainland, may be named for its elusive inhabitants. However, they are by no means the only avian species to roost on this island.

We were treated to a pelican flock's flyby. They flew in perfect formation before landing on a hill and standing around like a gaggle of teenagers busily chatting. A pair of Australian pied oystercatchers poked around the rocky shoreline with their neon orange beaks looking for a snack. And a group of Greater crested terns executed a perfect statue imitation. We weren't sure why they all faced northwest, perhaps to catch some extra rays or just avoid the wind.

Yet, it was the Silver Gulls that were the most noticeable, partly due to their numbers. There were hundreds of them. Everywhere. We were careful not to walk in the grass where the birds were obviously nesting. Nevertheless, our very presence unnerved them. One even dive bombed me and plucked the hat off my head, warning us to steer clear. Message received.

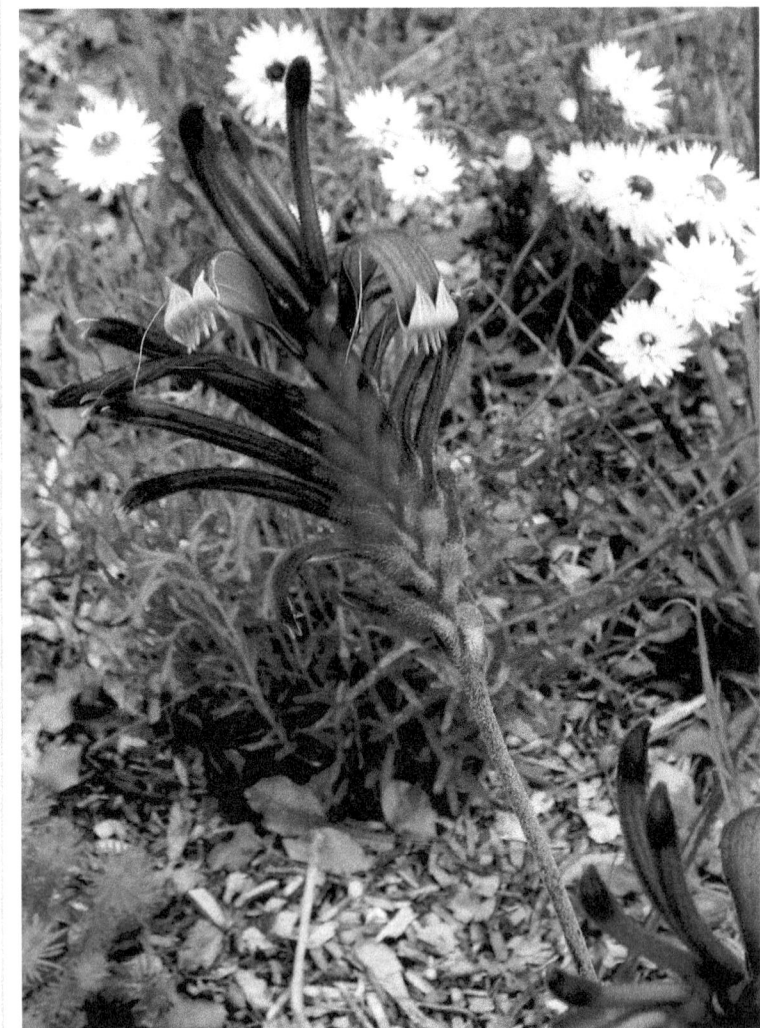

Contradictions in Nature

Oz is home to some of Earth's more unusual flora and fauna. Take for example the platypus. This comical creature defies rules. It's a semiaquatic mammal that lays eggs. And because there's nothing else like it, its uniqueness adds to what makes it fascinating.

Another remarkable Aussie is the Kangaroo Paw. What's intriguing about it is the fuzzy, braided stem from which tubular flowers branch off and a claw-like feature pops out at the end that resembles a kangaroo's paw. This distinctive plant was adopted as WA's emblem and is now exported from its native region extending from Kalbarri to Esperance to other parts of the world.

Similar to the platypus, the Kangaroo Paw has a notable contradictory characteristic. The fuzz on its flowers can irritate human skin. Nonetheless, extract from this plant has been used for centuries in Aboriginal medicines and recently has been added to skin creams to reactivate skin firmness and increase collagen output. Another one of Mother Nature's mysteries.

Sailing on Blue Topaz

Combine the land mass of Texas, California, Montana, New Mexico, Arizona, Nevada and Washington state and you have about one million square miles, the same as in Western Australia. What's interesting is that only 2.5 million people live in this vast area. That's the equivalent of how many reside in the greater San Antonio metropolitan area. This much space offers WA residents almost unlimited elbow room to play onshore and off.

Most of the state's towns sit either next to or relatively close to the Indian Ocean. Scientists say that the color of the water varies depending on how much sunlight can filter through the particles. Regardless of where we traveled up and down the coast, we were surprised to see that part or all of the ocean looked like a sparkling blue topaz.

A half-hour train ride south of Perth lies the beautiful seashore town of Mandurah. Comet Bay was a marvelous place to soak in the WA lifestyle, epitomized by this sailboat gliding along the ocean's endless ribbons of blue.

Meandering Through the
Margaret River Region

A Second Life

Few coastal towns are blessed like Fremantle with natural deep-water channels that allow shipping vessels to sail right to shore for an easy transfer of goods. To remedy this situation, some towns choose to build a pier. Busselton initially built a relatively modest timber pile jetty in 1864 that stretched 176 meters into the ocean. This was continually extended out to sea due to changes in water levels and ship size until it became the longest of its kind in the Southern Hemisphere.

Despite their efforts, city officials realized by 1972 that the jetty was no longer cost-effective to maintain and closed it to commercial ships. They considered tearing it down until the community stepped in to save the iconic structure as a tourist attraction. A track was placed on the 1,841-meter long pier, along with a pint-sized red train powered by 30 solar roof panels. Now, 500,000 passengers ride down the jetty every year to view the 300-plus marine species living in the natural underwater aquarium.

More Than a Place to Swim

Locals and tourists to the Margaret River region have a long list of nearby beaches to enjoy. In between Eagle Bay and Dunsborough lies Meelup Beach. This crescent shaped spot was named by the Wadandi people and means "place of the moon rising" since the moon gives the illusion of rising out of the ocean a few nights each year. It's well known for its calm, clear waters, ideal for swimmers and paddleboarders. And for landlubbers who don't want to get wet, there are plenty of jarrah trees to provide welcome shade from the Aussie sun.

It was late September when we visited and disappointingly too cool to go swimming. We took a stroll along the white sand instead and became fascinated by the outcroppings of granite boulders. They varied in size and appeared to pop out of the ground at a 45-degree angle. But what really caught our attention were the humpback whales breaching just off shore on their annual trek north to warmer waters. The chance to see their acrobatics was better than a swim.

Expressions in the Air

An excellent way to learn about a culture is through its architecture. A society's artistic tastes, styles and traditions are on full display in her buildings. Australia though is a paradox. Her Indigenous Aborigines have the oldest living cultural history on the planet dating back more than 50,000 years, yet there are no structures more than 200 years old.

While the country may be a newbie to the architectural scene by Eastern or Mid-Eastern Standards, she has quickly learned that it provides her citizens with a permanent form of expression. And one of the more unusual ways they let their personalities shine through is with their choice of weathervanes.

Similar to other countries, Oz has its share of ubiquitous roosters atop barns, houses and city halls. We also saw several ornaments affixed to spinning compass points that were quintessentially Australian. Yallingup, along the coast, was home to our favorite. This one exudes the palpable Aussie enthusiasm and their love of water sports.

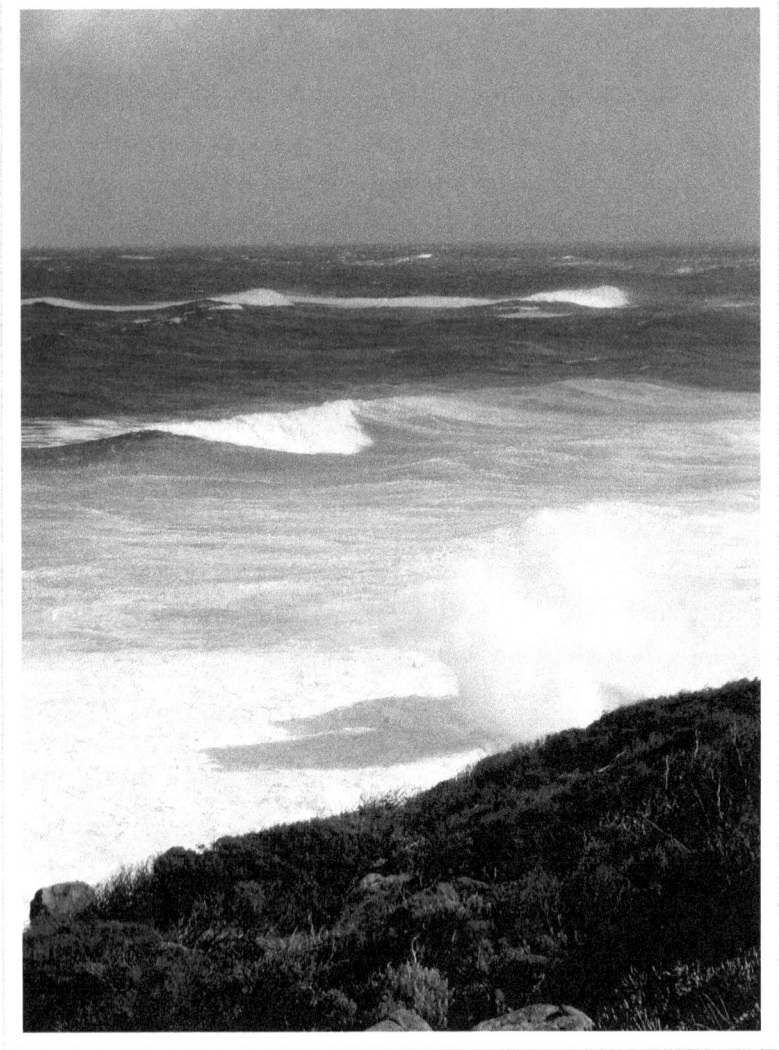

Sticky Beak

For most Aussies, the ideal day at the beach has a simple formula. Take some bright blue skies. Don't forget your sunnies (sunglasses), hat, bathers (swimsuit) and sunscreen. Throw in several coldies (cold drinks). Add in a large space to spread out your towel to read, nap or build a sand castle. Then jump in the ocean for a quick swim to cool off. Perfect.

However, the coast can also offer something special on those days that may appear less than idyllic, specifically drama. Seafoam appears whipped and thick. The water gradually turns from blue to an icy grey. And the waves relentlessly pound the shore, some shooting several stories skywards.

Sticky Beak Point sits just outside of Gracetown. This overlook earned its name not from any native bird, but the Aussie term referring to a person who puts his nose where it doesn't belong. As we stood cliffside, peering over the edge, we understood how appropriate the name was. We took a couple of steps backwards to safely watch the ocean's show.

Stylish Camouflage

Several members of the animal kingdom can only be found in the Land Down Under. Some of them are adorable and cuddly, like the koala. However, the coastal taipan which is a highly venomous snake, not so much.

One or more of the four sub-species of Australian Ringneck parrots can be seen flying around the country, except for Tasmania or the far north. The 28 in Western Australia was named such because residents claim its call sounds like the words, "Twenty-eight." No matter how many times or how closely we listened, we only heard bird chirps, nothing resembling words.

Most green parrots perch among a tree's branches and use the leaves or vines to help camouflage themselves. Yet, this 28 artfully blended in with the grass and spring wildflowers while foraging for its breakfast near the Ellensbrook homestead. Since 28s are known for their gregarious nature, maybe this one wasn't trying to hide from us, but rather show off how well his feathery outfit color coordinated with his surroundings.

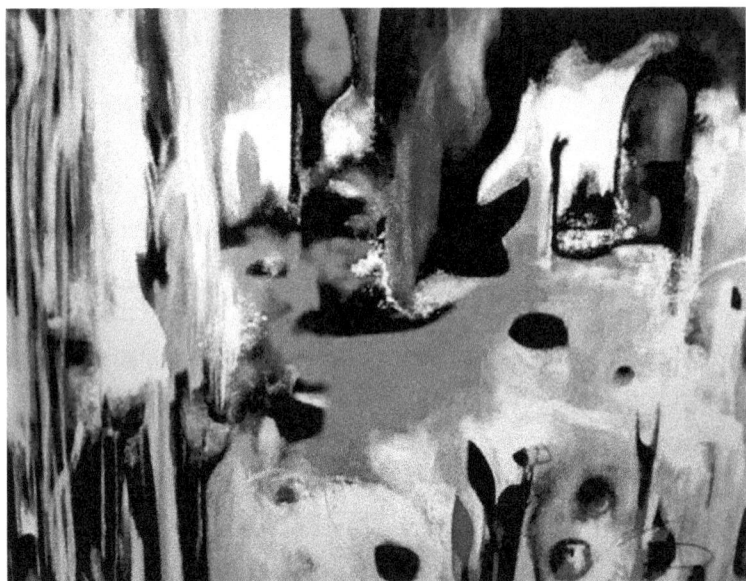

The Art of Wine

The Margaret River area is synonymous for wine country in WA. Though grapes have been dangling from vines here since the settlers first planted them back in the 1830s, the industry didn't take off until the late 1960s.

One of the earliest vineyards was the Leeuwin Estate, owned by the Horgan family who completely transformed an old cattle station into one of the region's most beautiful wineries. Its gentle rolling hills were ideal to grow grapes that produce award-winning Cabernet Sauvignon, Chardonnay, Shiraz and Pinot Noir wines.

However, we discovered this place is known for more than viticulture. It also features a gourmet restaurant overlooking manicured gardens where kookaburras laugh. And one more thing makes a drive to this estate worthwhile. They have a fantastic modern art gallery with over 150 paintings by Australian artists. Many of these works of art have been showcased on the winery's labels for its premium vintages known as the Art Series. The best part? Admission is free.

A Place of Silence

Tucked into the southwestern corner of the state is a unique attraction. There are no neon signs pointing the way. There wasn't even a ticket booth to pay an entrance fee. We simply drove right in.

It was quiet the spring morning we entered the Karri forest. Other than a few birds who whistled brief tunes, there was almost complete silence. About the only sound other than our footsteps was the muffled patter of raindrops on the wild calla lilies covering the forest floor.

It was extraordinary to walk among these giants. We cranked our necks back to peer at the tops of this eucalyptus species that's deemed one of the tallest hardwoods. Yet, it was more than their height that took our breaths away. This forest is the only one with this type of tree—not just in the state, not just in Australia, but in the world. There are so few spots where it can be said something's replicated nowhere else. The opportunity to wander through such a special place made us feel like we were on hallowed ground.

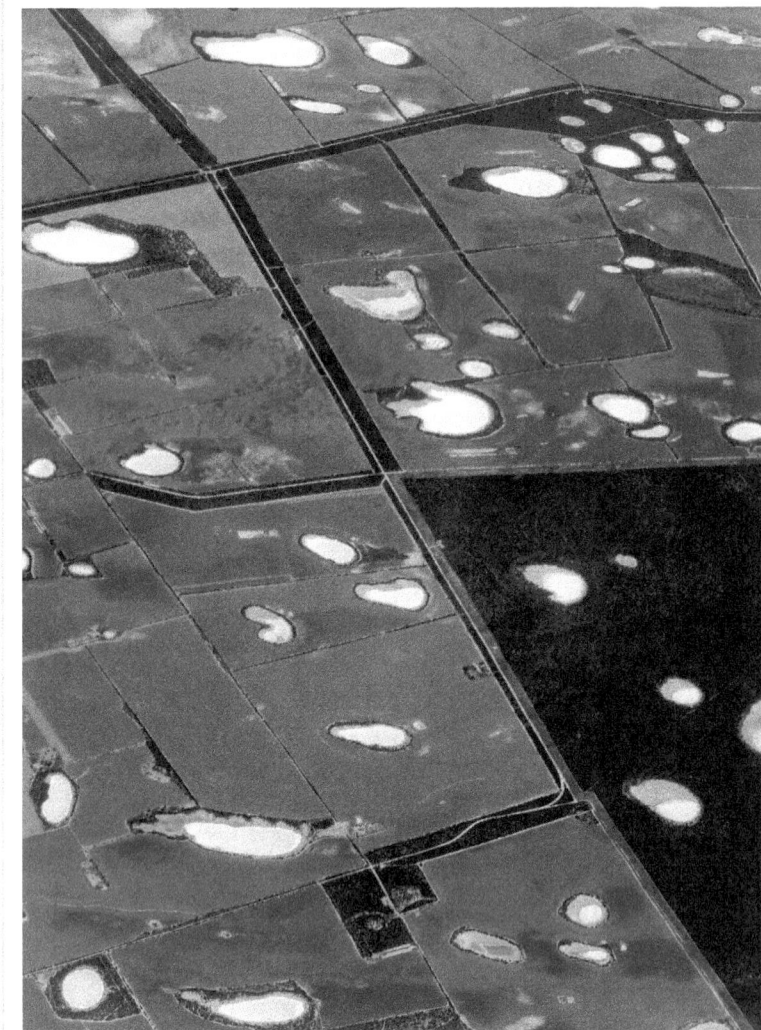

Some Grains and Salt

We booked two window seats to travel from Perth to Melbourne. Then we crossed our fingers that it'd be cloud-free when we flew so that the trip would be like a multi-hour aerial tour (without commentary) offering a different perspective.

One of the most intriguing views was over the southwestern corner of the state. It was easy to see why this region was nicknamed the Wheat Belt. Roads crisscrossed massive squares and rectangles of crops. Yet, there was also something odd. The land was pocked with colossal white and yellow splotches, resembling an abstract painting.

These salt lakes of varying shapes and sizes are the result of the early settlers' good intentions to clear vast areas of native vegetation. While the removal of the deep-rooting plants allowed for expansive fields, it resulted in giant subterranean salt deposits surfacing when the water table rose because no large plants were left to absorb the rainfall. Now farmers do their best to work with the soil rather than against it.

The Authors

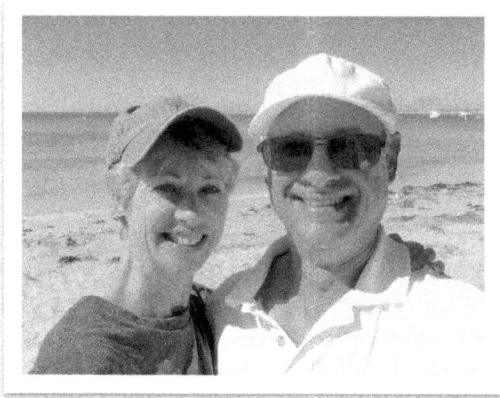

The two of us were bitten by the travel bug at the very beginning of our marriage when we chose to have a small wedding and a big honeymoon. That 10-week adventure took us through western Europe. Thirty-five years later, we've visited 20 countries and 38 American states. Every new destination is a chance to immerse ourselves in another culture and an opportunity to share our experiences through our writing and photographs.

We'd like to thank you for purchasing our book and hope that you found it both entertaining and enlightening. It's been a fun challenge to write our impressions about the places we visited following our theme, *A Picture Is Worth 1,000 Characters*.

following our theme, A Picture Is Worth 1,000 Characters.

Please check out the other books in our series that are in paperback featuring black and white photographs and as e-books with color photos. If you enjoyed this one, we encourage you to write a review on the online retailer's site where you purchased it. Also, don't forget to visit our website at www.imaginexxus.com to read other stories about our journeys.

Bon voyage,
MacKenzie and Doug